way the way we view this issue in a way that has the potential to improve the quality of life for millions of people.

JACK MARKELL
Governor of Delaware

Randy Lewis has forever changed employment practices. With his vision and commitment, businesses from around the world can see recruiting people with disabilities as hiring people's ability and benefiting the company's bottom line.

CHET COOPER
Founder of ABILITYJobs.com and publisher of *ABILITY* magazine

When it comes to monumental, attitudinal, start-a-movement consequences in the world of business, I don't know anyone who has accomplished what Randy Lewis has. In his new book, he shares an intensely personal story of heart, home, work, faith, doubt, and courage. The book begins with the birth of their autistic son and ends with Randy's role in leading Walgreens—the world's largest drugstore chain—to become the global model in proving that disabled employees in large numbers not only match but often exceed their peers in the workplace. This is a compelling, insightful, compassionate account that most of us won't believe until we read it. Here is an amazing feat of faith and foresight come true—an account full of steadiness and inspiration, a drumbeat to victory over insurmountable odds, a moral tale well told—that demonstrates an incomparable love that can develop between so-called haves and have-nots.

ALLAN COX
CEO counselor and author of *Change the Way You Face the Day*

This is a book about the transforming power of love—the love of a father for his son, certainly, but also the genuine love that can flow well beyond the bonds of family or kinship to effect transformation in entire structures in business and the wider society. Randy Lewis shows us how faith and love can be put into practice to make this world a more just and compassionate place . . . and be good business, to boot.

JEFFREY D. LEE
Episcopal bishop of Chicago

Randy helped one of the nation's landmark companies to see, and seize, the chance to employ an underappreciated—and too often misunderstood—workforce, challenge old myths and assumptions, advance our culture, and set an example for others. Best of all, he showed that we should never overlook or underestimate anyone who wants to contribute to our nation's economy and better their lives along the way. In doing so, Randy underscored a valuable lesson about doing good by doing good business.

GREG WASSON
CEO of Walgreens

Randy Lewis is a pioneer, demonstrating through his efforts at Walgreens that people with disabilities, given the chance and the tools, will succeed. By harnessing the power of business and the longing in each of us to make a difference, he has done what many thought impossible. This is a must-read for corporate leaders.

MARCA BRISTO
President of Access Living, former chair on the National Council on Disability

A bold and courageous story—essential rightness exemplified. An inspiring read for business leaders, a heartwarming read for parents, and a must-read anyone facing a challenge.

JOHAN AURIK
Managing partner and chairman of the board, A.T. Kearney

Possessed with passion and skill, Randy Lewis spearheaded the effort to transform Walgreens distribution facilities into a work environment that was welcoming, inclusive, and supportive of people with disabilities. This book tells this touching and moving story—one that is both highly personal and extremely

Fascinating. This book should be required reading in every business school to teach future business leaders that hiring people with disabilities and making innovations in the workplace are both good business and the right thing to do.

TEMPLE GRANDIN
Author of *Thinking in Pictures* and *The Autistic Brain*

Randy Lewis is a real trailblazer. He never forgot his community during his very successful business years. This book is a real eye-opener. He put his career on the line to demonstrate that serving the needs of the community also serves the needs of business. When you do both together, you really have achieved success.

BOB WRIGHT
Cofounder of Autism Speaks, former vice chairman of General Electric Company, former chairman and CEO of NBC Universal

Unconditional love, unending patience, and total dedication to a good cause create miracles. What a better world we would have following Randy's example.

C. R. WALGREEN III
Chairman emeritus, Walgreens Company

A powerful story! This book should be adopted as a must-read in all MBA programs in order to inspire leaders of consequence. Randy's story proves that leading with heart is the only way to lead.

THOMAS F. KELLER
Dean Emeritus of the Fuqua School of Business at Duke University

It was a privilege to attend the grand opening of the distribution plant in Anderson, South Carolina. Many employees, almost all of them disabled, told me of their great affection for and gratitude toward Randy. His support of their abilities to help Walgreens as employees of the company provides them self-confidence, growth, and a future as productive citizens. This book reveals the path Randy followed to his incredible success in the corporate world and highlights how much his success is rooted in family and faith. Few executives have done what Randy has accomplished, but all of us can use him as a role model for superior, contemporary leadership. I am a better person for knowing him and his family and calling them friends.

JANET HILL
Member, boards of directors of Wendy's, Dean Foods, Echo360, and the Carlyle Group

This is a beautiful book linking personal experience and trauma to constructive efforts to provide those with disabilities opportunities to participate in the mainstream. This is a story with great poignancy that will convince you through both your heart and your brain.

HERBERT PARDES, MD
Executive vice chairman of the board of trustees, NewYork–Presbyterian

This is the story of a company, its leader, and its workforce changing the world for thousands of people with disabilities. It is a story that should inspire us all.

SENATOR TOM HARKIN

I'm convinced we all have a purpose in life. Randy Lewis's story is one of how purpose, compassion, and commitment to excellence have taught ordinary people to do the extraordinary. He is truly changing the world.

STEVE SZILAGYI
Supply chain executive, Lowe's Companies, Inc.

Randy Lewis offers valuable lessons for building a better society, demonstrating the tremendous value of focusing on people's abilities, not their disabilities. Having traveled across the country for discussions about how to address the persistently high rate of unemployment for people with disabilities, I can confidently state that no one makes a more powerful case than Randy that hiring these individuals isn't about charity; it's good for the bottom line. Thanks in large part to his leadership, Walgreens is changing the professional—in Randy's own words. Building on a successful heritage, Randy courageously led his team into uncharted yet extremely rewarding territory by integrating hardworking but humbled people yearning for purpose and eager to contribute. The results are thrilling. It is a wonderful story to read and witness.

WILLIAM C. FOOTE
Retired chairman and CEO of USG Corporation

Randy Lewis has led a truly remarkable life. There is much we can learn from everything he has done in the workplace and at home. I loved this book—it is a must-read, chock-full of great advice on how to make a difference and inspire others to do great things.

NELSON PELTZ
Founding partner and CEO of Trian Fund Management, L.P.

If you are looking for a way to inspire your team and make yours a better company, this book is a must-read. Inspired by experiences with his autistic son, Randy Lewis used solid business principles and innovational techniques to improve productivity by leveraging the unique talents of the disabled. In the process, he brought real meaning to the work and lives of thousands.

DAVID W. BERNAUER
Retired CEO of Walgreens

No Greatness without Goodness is an inspirational story. Randy, with ease and integrity, did the right thing in business, and everyone involved—from stakeholders to the disadvantaged—came out as winners. This book is about triumph, not just in the corporate world, but especially in the lives of people with disabilities.

PAUL HOUSE
Chairman of Tim Hortons

Randy Lewis changed the way we see the world in this superb book, as he guides us in a passionate new way to see Austin's potential. As he tells his remarkable story of *No Greatness without Goodness* to my classes, he inspires students to give of themselves for returns they can receive for their whole lives.

PROFESSOR HOWARD HAAS
University of Chicago

A heartwarming account of how one man's vision inspired many, from business leaders to frontline employees, to unlock the true mission and meaning of success in industry and in life.

JEFF KELLAN
Vice president of distribution, Toys"R"Us

A remarkable and inspiring story of how a father learned some of life's most important lessons from his autistic son and launched a revolution in career opportunities for the disabled. Sprinkled throughout with humor and wisdom, this is the "feel good" book of the year, and the best part is that it's all true.

WILLIAM E. KIRWAN
Chancellor, University System of Maryland

No Greatness without Goodness describes the power and impact of one person. Randy Lewis's love of his child changed corporate human resources strategy forever. The ability of a major corporation to enhance the lives of people often in the shadows is exhilarating and shows that one of the most important roles of corporate leaders is to create an environment where every person can reach their full potential.

NANCY M. SCHLICHTING
CEO of Henry Ford Health System, director of Walgreens Company

An extraordinary story of the power of the human spirit of one man and how Randy Lewis's unconditional love for his autistic son emboldened him to change Walgreens' workplace forever. In doing so, he has given hope to thousands with disabilities. Anything seems possible after reading *No Greatness without Goodness*.

EMIL BROLICK
CEO of Wendy's

NO GREATNESS WITHOUT GOODNESS

HOW A FATHER'S LOVE CHANGED A COMPANY AND SPARKED A MOVEMENT

RANDY LEWIS

RET Walgreens Senior Vice President

LION

To Kay, of course

Text copyright © 2014 J. Randolph Lewis

The right of J. Randolph Lewis to be identified as the author of this work has been asserted by him in accordance with the Copyright, Designs and Patents Act 1988.

Published by Lion Books
an imprint of
Lion Hudson plc
Wilkinson House, Jordan Hill Road,
Oxford OX2 8DR, England
www.lionhudson.com/lion

ISBN 978 0 7459 5618 3
e-ISBN 978 0 7459 5779 1

Published in association with the literary agency of Mendel Media Group LLC, 115 West 30th Street, Suite 800, New York, NY 10001.

Acknowledgments
Cover and author photographs by Stephen Vosloo, copyright © 2013 by Tyndale House Publishers. All rights reserved.

Designed by Jacqueline L. Nuñez

Edited by Stephanie Rische

Unless otherwise indicated, all Scripture quotations are taken from the Holy Bible, New Living Translation, copyright © 1996, 2004, 2007, 2013 by Tyndale House Foundation. Used by permission of Tyndale House Publishers, Inc., Carol Stream, Illinois 60188. All rights reserved.

Some of the names have been changed out of respect for the privacy of the individuals mentioned in this book.

A catalogue record for this book is available from the British Library

Printed and bound in the UK, April 2014, LH26

Contents

CHAPTER 1   Thank You and Yes   *1*

CHAPTER 2   Go with the Terrain   *9*

CHAPTER 3   Connecting   *19*

CHAPTER 4   Finding Gold in Dark Places   *23*

CHAPTER 5   Be Ready   *29*

CHAPTER 6   Archimedes and the Scorpion   *33*

CHAPTER 7   Money, Mission, and Meaning   *41*

CHAPTER 8   Principles Require Action   *47*

CHAPTER 9   Find the Crack in the Concrete   *51*

CHAPTER 10   Playing Chess   *55*

CHAPTER 11   Failure Is Just a Time-Out   *59*

CHAPTER 12   Compassion and Justice   *63*

CHAPTER 13   Adjusting Our Sails   *71*

CHAPTER 14   Pick Your Moment   *75*

CHAPTER 15   Best Practices   *83*

CHAPTER 16   Leaders Go before Their Troops   *89*

CHAPTER 17   I'd Better See Some Dinosaurs   *93*

CHAPTER 18   Manage Your Fear   *95*

CHAPTER 19   Cash in Your Chips   *99*

CHAPTER 20   Cathedral Builders   *103*

CHAPTER 21   Crossing the Rubicon   *107*

CHAPTER 22   Eliminate Fear   *111*

CHAPTER 23   Share the Story   *115*

CHAPTER 24   Where the Buck Stops   *121*

CHAPTER 25   The Journey Is Worth It   *125*

CHAPTER 26   Bucking the Status Quo   *129*

CHAPTER 27   Don't Let the Big One Get Away *133*

CHAPTER 28   Esther's Lesson *139*

CHAPTER 29   The World Is Waiting *143*

CHAPTER 30   Katrina *147*

CHAPTER 31   Manage in the Gray *151*

CHAPTER 32   Share the Load *155*

CHAPTER 33   Sacagaweas *159*

CHAPTER 34   Tough Love *167*

CHAPTER 35   Failure Is Not an Option *171*

CHAPTER 36   Breathing Life into the Dream *175*

CHAPTER 37   Positive Distractions *181*

CHAPTER 38   Clear and Elevating Goals *185*

CHAPTER 39   Verily, Verily *191*

CHAPTER 40   Being Andrew *195*

CHAPTER 41   A Place to Succeed *201*

CHAPTER 42   How Long? *209*

Acknowledgments *213*

APPENDIX 1   Principles for Hiring People with Disabilities *217*

APPENDIX 2   Moving from Grief to Acceptance *223*

Notes *227*

About the Author *229*

CHAPTER I

THANK YOU AND YES

*Never doubt that a small group of thoughtful, committed citizens can change
the world. Indeed, it is the only thing that ever has.*

MARGARET MEAD

I HAD PRACTICED my speech over and over, but I was still nervous as I climbed the stairs to the stage in the middle of the Paris Las Vegas ballroom. Surrounded by an audience of five thousand Walgreens store managers, I said that we were about to undertake something that had never been done before—anywhere. We were planning to build the most efficient distribution center of its kind in the world.

And we were going to staff one-third of the workforce with people who have disabilities, many of whom had never been offered a job. People with mental disabilities such as autism and cognitive delays. People with physical disabilities such as cerebral palsy, epilepsy, spinal cord injuries, and missing limbs. We were going to pay them the same as people without disabilities, have them perform the same jobs, and hold them to the same standards. We would offer full benefits and full-time employment, taking hundreds of people off welfare rolls.

And then Walgreens would do something else we'd never done: we would open our doors to the world—even our competitors—and share everything we'd learned with them.

As I prepared to tell the five thousand store managers how we were going to do all this, the huge screens surrounding the stage filled with a picture of my family. That's because my family is where the story began.

Under a gorgeous full moon, not long before dawn on Friday the 13th of May in 1988, my wife, Kay, and I drove toward the hospital and into a future more frightening, more humbling, and more wondrous than anything we could have imagined.

Apparently full moons don't just bring out werewolves, as all the labor rooms were taken. After four hours of labor on a gurney in the hallway, Kay delivered our son into the world. He didn't make a sound. His silence surprised me—his older sister had been born wailing, but our boy didn't even whimper. Still attached to his mom, he gazed into his new world, content to leave the commotion to others.

Our dreams for our second child were of the ordinary kind—baseball, Cub Scouts, model airplanes—but we would soon learn that this was no ordinary child. None of those childhood pleasures were to be his. Instead, he was to be my catalyst, my inspiration, and my goad. He would compel me toward action that I never would have thought possible.

I would like to say that my son looked like me, but mostly he just looked like any other chubby, healthy, happy baby born that day. In keeping with my roots, I had placed a small bag of Texas dirt under his mother's hospital bed in Barrington, Illinois, so one day he could claim that he'd been born on Texas soil. As we'd been planning even before we were married, Kay and I named him Austin, after the capital city of my home state. It was a good day.

In the following months, Austin progressed as expected, losing those chubby cheeks but not his beautiful smile. He crawled and learned to walk as he morphed from a baby to a toddler. Once he could walk, he was fast and curious. He terrorized Kay by slipping away during so many shopping trips that she began to tell store managers he was deaf so they would join the search for him. Austin's younger sister, Allison, was born eighteen months after he was, so with three kids in less than five years, we had a hectic but seemingly ordinary life.

Ordinary, that is, until the weekend we took the family to Kentucky for a reunion with Kay's relatives. I spent most of the weekend with two-year-old Austin on my shoulders, which was the only way I could keep him from sprinting away. It was a satisfactory arrangement for both of us. If I carried him, I didn't have to worry that he'd run off. And Austin was content to communicate his needs by twisting my head whichever direction he wanted to go.

Kay's family is full of schoolteachers, and as they watched her deal with a little boy who paid no attention to her praise or her scolding, they saw something we hadn't seen. And so began a lot of hushed conversations that would continue around us—but unheard by us—throughout the weekend. Kay's mother called soon after we returned home to suggest that our son ought to be tested for autism. Kay was so angry that she hung up without saying good-bye—something she'd never done before. The next week her mom sent us a book on autism. Angry with the kind of rage born of deep fear, Kay put it on the nightstand in the guest room without opening it. It sat there for a year.

Before his second birthday, Austin had been using some words: *Daddy. Bye-bye. No.* But now he seemed to be saying them less often. Kay's anxious eyes were assessing him all the time. His face seemed to have lost the quick expressions it once had. He paid so little heed to us that we suspected he might have truly gone deaf. We got his hearing tested, and although it was fine, Kay continued to worry. I'm the kind of guy who naturally thinks everything's going to be fine, and I told her to stop worrying. But she couldn't. After weeks of listening to her fret, I gave in.

"All right," I said. "Let's get him checked out. At least that will get everyone off our backs."

Before we took Austin in for testing, the doctor sent us assessment forms to fill out. As Kay went through the speech and language questions, she realized how much we had failed to notice. Words that Austin had once used—*ball, dog, water*—had disappeared entirely from his vocabulary.

"When did your child begin putting words together?" we read on the assessment form.

He hadn't yet. Not even two words. When Austin wanted something, he pointed or pulled us toward whatever he wanted. When we couldn't understand him, he cried and threw tantrums.

As we sat in the specialist's waiting room a few days after Austin had completed the comprehensive battery of tests, I was planning the grief I'd give Kay's family when the tests showed our son to be perfectly fine. As we walked into the doctor's office, I expected to hear that Austin's speech was a little delayed, which is common in boys, and that he'd grow out of it.

Kay joked with the doctor as we shook his hand. "So, you're going to tell me that I feed him too much sugar, aren't you?"

The doctor didn't smile. Instead, he said, "Why don't you have a seat, and let's go over what we found."

Almost every test showed that Austin lagged far behind expectations. He had delays with language—both understanding and speech—and problems with motor skills and muscle tone. The doctor said our son had pervasive development disorder, which was often code for autism in those days. No one knew the cause of Austin's condition. Hoping for a silver lining, I asked, "Will he get better as he grows older?"

The doctor glanced up from the reports before him, looked at both of us, and said quietly, "He might get worse."

Nightmare visions of our future flashed before me—putting locks on the doors and windows to keep our son from running away, changing diapers on a grown man, having to subdue an adult who threw tantrums like a two-year-old. A dozen other possibilities, each worse than the one before, filled my mind.

As Kay and I walked toward the car, I regained a bit of my usual optimism. Things had turned out differently than we'd hoped. But problems are for solving. I had a good salary and medical insurance. I tried to cheer Kay up by reminding her that we still had a lot to be grateful for.

"Isn't it better for this to happen to us than to another family that doesn't have the love and resources we have?" I asked.

Kay wasn't with me on that one. Looking up toward a cloudless sky, she asked, "How can the sun be shining today?"

Once in the car, Kay began to cry—more than cry, actually. She began to sob like a child. I stared straight ahead, gripping the steering wheel until my fingers ached. A clock had begun ticking in my mind—the same clock that ticks in the mind of every parent with a child who has a disability. It marks off the minutes I have left in this world before I die and leave my son without someone to take care of him.

The son we had when we walked into that doctor's office was gone, just as surely as if he'd stopped breathing and died. The people Kay and I once were had died too. We'd been among the lucky ones. A happy marriage. A stable income. Three healthy children. The present was good, and we'd had every reason to think the future would be even better.

Now everything was different. We had joined the ranks of parents whose fate evokes pity and fear. Someone sent us a poem that I later learned is often sent to parents of children born with a disability.

Disability isn't another country; it's another world.

Called "Welcome to Holland," the poem is written from the perspective of a person who has his heart set on visiting Paris and spends months in joyous anticipation and planning. But his plane is diverted to Holland instead. After his initial disappointment, the traveler learns to appreciate what Holland has to offer that Paris doesn't—tulips, windmills, Rembrandt.

The poem was sent to comfort us. It didn't.

We weren't in another country; we were in another world. We'd expected to land on Earth, but we'd ended up on Mars—an arid, desolate, lonely world where nothing relating to our son would ever be easy again. We'd struggle in ways others wouldn't be able to imagine, and we'd be judged by people who couldn't possibly understand our situation. Restaurants, shops, theaters—all the places we'd once enjoyed with our children—would become sites of such anxiety when our son was present that we would stay away. Friends who had once welcomed us and our children would now reassess their invitations. If you think people don't like it when you bring your dog to their house, try bringing your autistic child.

We were given Austin's diagnosis on the Wednesday. Two nights later, at the Good Friday service, Kay sang with a septet during the evening service. As she stood at the front of the church, with the cross before her and the baptismal font behind her, she sang her heart out. There was only one question on her heart: *God, what have you called us to?*

We blamed ourselves; we blamed factors outside ourselves. But we never blamed God. Even so, we didn't understand why this was happening. If God had some grand design in sending us Austin, we couldn't see it. All we could see was the back of the quilt—the mess of loose ends and tied-off threads you find on the homely undersides of old-fashioned quilts. If he was using us to piece together a brilliant pattern, it was facing away from us, far from our own line of vision.

Kay and I began to scrutinize our pasts for anything we might have done that could have caused harm to our son. In the years to come, we would hear that mothers of children with autism were once blamed for not giving their babies the early nurturing they needed. Refrigerator mothers, they'd been called. Had we neglected Austin when he was a baby? No. Not intentionally—never. Kay adored and enjoyed our children, even under the most trying of circumstances. She'd nursed Austin until he was a year old. He'd been a normal, affectionate baby.

Then he changed. At one point we read that some people blame immunizations for autism. We retraced our steps and concluded that Austin had begun losing his language at about the same time he got his immunizations. Should we have skipped the immunizations? The research indicated there was no direct link to autism, but we were scrounging for answers.

We had no idea what lay ahead. In my grade school *Weekly Reader*, I'd read about Dag Hammarskjöld, the secretary general of the United Nations. Then, years later, I heard a simple but beautiful prayer he wrote. It had sunk into the cobwebs of my mind until the day of the doctor's visit, when it burst to the surface. The next morning I went into my office, found the prayer, printed it out, and pinned it on my cubicle wall, where I saw it every time I sat down at my desk. It was the best expression of hope I could muster.

For all that has been, thank you.
For all that will be, yes.

CHAPTER 2

GO WITH THE TERRAIN

BEFORE AUSTIN'S BIRTH, we knew only enough about autism to be afraid of it. When couples are expecting, the typical question they're asked is "Are you hoping for a boy or a girl?" The rote answer is "Either, as long as the baby is healthy." Kay and I felt that way about each of our children as we awaited their births. We had both a boy's name and a girl's name ready. With our firstborn, we had been fully expecting a boy. So when our daughter arrived, I exclaimed to Kay in joy and surprise, "It's Sarah!" Three years later, I announced Austin in the same fashion.

Occasionally during her pregnancy, Kay and I mused about the possibility that our soon-to-be-born child might have a problem. When we asked ourselves what disability we most feared, we answered, "Autism." Everything we knew about autism came from a popular TV show at the time called *St. Elsewhere*, which featured a character whose son, Tommy, had autism. Although Tommy was about ten, he didn't speak. He got frustrated easily and threw things. He didn't like to be touched, and nobody in the family knew how to communicate with him.

Austin had none of those traits at first. And then, seemingly out of nowhere, he did. When he quit talking at around fifteen months, it was as though he'd lost all means of communication. If he was thirsty, he would grab Kay's hand, take her to the refrigerator, and put her hand on the door to open it. She'd open the refrigerator and say, "What, honey? What do you want?" He couldn't talk or even point but would simply fall on the floor crying because Kay couldn't figure out if he wanted juice or milk. The emotional level in our house was almost unbearable.

After our initial shock at Austin's diagnosis, we met with the doctor again to understand what we could do to help Austin. Knowing the impact a disability can have on the family dynamic, he suggested that the first order of business was to get Austin's behavior under control. We were given an intensive six-week intervention plan. It was work. It was tedious. It required constant monitoring. And it saved our lives.

One of the first tasks was to determine what Austin did and did not understand. Then we needed to reinforce the idea of compliance. For the first week, Kay walked around with a little notebook and made observations about whether or not Austin complied with a request. Each page had two columns. If she asked him to do something and he didn't comply, she checked the noncompliance column. If he complied after three asks or fewer, he got a check in the compliance column. That first week was a huge eye-opener. It showed us in black and white how little impact our words had. We'd suspected it, but we hadn't charted it. Seeing the pattern we'd been living out was sobering.

In week two, we gave Austin one Skittle every time he complied. After a request, we were to audibly count to three, and if he complied before we got to three, he received the Skittle. If he didn't, no Skittle. He really wanted that candy, and he quickly came to expect that counting meant candy. The first time Kay made it to three and refused to hand over the Skittle, he was furious. That was a tantrum to remember, but Kay stayed strong. In a relatively short period of time, the little boy who could never seem to hear us was starting to understand remarkably well.

In week three we stepped it up a bit by bringing in the missing piece—time-outs. Austin continued to receive a Skittle for compliance, but now with noncompliance he had to sit in a chair in the corner of the dining room for three minutes. Consistency was essential. Every time he didn't comply, he had to go to time-out. No matter what was going on. No matter where we were. Every time.

At first Kay resisted. Three minutes seemed too long, especially when Austin's infractions came one after another, all day long. The doctor reminded her that a time-out was not a lack of parental love but a lack of parental attention. If Austin continued to get the reward of our attention for doing things we didn't like, he would have no reason to do what we asked of him. Our son was autistic, but he wasn't stupid. Once Kay could see the time-outs as nurturing rather than depriving, she fully committed to the program.

Time-outs became our life. We learned that three minutes is plenty—that two time-outs of three minutes each is much more valuable than a single ten-minute time-out. Fortunately, our little boy would sit in the chair. We'd simply say, "Time-out" and walk with Austin to the dining room, where he would sit while the timer ticked away. When the bell rang, he got up and went about his business. If he tried to leave early, we would sit him back down and rewind the timer so he knew it had started over, and there would be no credit for time served. The time-outs were so effective that eventually Austin would grab my hands or put his hand over my mouth as soon as I began to count to three.

This structured system of discipline was a gift to our whole family. We now had a language to use with our nonverbal son. We were all happier. It was such an effective system that Kay also applied it to the girls. They had their charts on the refrigerator, and they received stars for compliance. When they got ten stars, they received some Skittles. It was a win for everyone.

That summer, on our yearly two-week vacation to Myrtle Beach, South Carolina, we were still very much entrenched in our program. There were so many time-outs that Kay and I played Rock, Paper, Scissors to see who would take Austin off the beach, trudge back to the condo, go up the elevator to the eighth floor, and sit with him while he had a time-out in the dining room. Kay's mother, who spent a week with us, said, "Austin seems to be spending half his vacation in a time-out." It may have seemed like it, but we kept at it, knowing we were making progress.

Back home in the suburbs of Chicago, with three children under the age of five and far from relatives who might have helped out, those next few years were hard, lonely ones for Kay. Even the smallest pleasures could be curtailed by our son's difficulties. Austin almost never made it through a restaurant meal without having a meltdown. As other parents watched Kay struggle with our screaming son, she felt their disapproval and judgment. She was never safe, even at home.

She would dress Austin in the morning and then turn her attention to Sarah or Allison, only to have our son disappear. If he was in the house and heard her calling, he didn't respond. One morning, when city workers were repaving the street outside the house, Kay came out of the shower to find that Austin had vanished. As she ran through room after room searching for him, she glanced out the window. Although the doors were always locked, he'd managed to get outside and was walking in his socks through molten tar that had just been laid on the street.

Austin's escapes from our house were frequent enough that Kay often walked the neighborhood with the two girls, one in tow, the other in a stroller, calling his name. One day as she pulled the girls along, she thought with despair, *This can't go on. It's ruining the girls' lives.* The next day an anonymous note was in our mailbox. It read, "If you can't keep the kid, I will." Kay called me in a panic. I came home, and we called the police. Some of our neighbors knew about Austin's difficulties, and others didn't. Had one of them written the note? What did "I will" mean? We didn't know. And we couldn't just let it sit.

I decided to write our neighbors a letter addressing the message we'd received. My letter began with the words, "Our son, Austin, is autistic. . . ." We put a copy in every mailbox in the neighborhood. Some of our neighbors called us to tell us how outraged they were about the note we'd received. One father came to our door offering whatever help we needed. We never found out who wrote the note, but we never got another one.

This incident served as a reminder for us to redouble our efforts to integrate Austin into family life and to help him fit into the world. Language, specifically language processing, is a common struggle for those with autism, and we knew it would play a key role in his being able to live a normal life. Knowing words and saying them are not nearly as difficult as knowing what they mean—not to mention how they relate to each other in the real world.

Among the experiences Kay and I most yearned for was a real, normal, back-and-forth conversation with Austin. Even just one, just once. We were comforted by those "If you don't laugh, you'll go crazy" conversations with other parents when we joked that it felt as if we were in an episode of *Star Trek*. If only we could perform the Vulcan mind-meld that allowed Mr. Spock to read thoughts by placing his hands on each side of someone's head. More than once, I would actually put my hands gently on each side of my sleeping son's head, thinking, *If I could only know what you're thinking*. I often prayed, *God, please let me know what's going on in there. Is he afraid? Is he happy? What does he want? What will help him?*

An electrician who came to work on our house when Austin was young recognized the cause of Austin's behavior because he had seen the same thing in his own autistic daughter. As his work stretched through the morning and into the afternoon, Kay made lunch for him. As they ate, she asked, "Have you ever had a conversation with your daughter?"

"No," he replied. "I dream that someday we will."

That night when I came home, Kay said, "For the first time, I felt as if someone understood what we're going through. It meant so much to me just to be a little less lonely." Austin is now in his twenties, and we still have never had a normal conversation with him. Maybe that's something that awaits us on the other side of this life.

Austin might never have learned to communicate as well as he does now if it hadn't been for his younger sister. Allison, born less than two years after Austin, was like his talking counterpart. Where Austin lacked in language, Allison excelled.

Allison became the number-one assistant for Austin's speech therapist. Austin attended weekly language therapy lessons, and Allison went with him to every session from the time she was born until she was old enough to stay at home by herself. She became known among the staff as the "co-therapist."

Watching Austin's therapy was like watching a martian (Austin) and an earthling (the therapist). The earthling was curious about the martian and tried to engage him. But to the martian, the earthling was just another part of the scenery, different only in that she made a lot of noise. Allison eventually became Austin's earthling interpreter.

It seemed as if our lives had been blown off course and we had crash-landed in uncharted territory.

Raising Austin was truly a family affair. Case in point: potty training. Austin was still using diapers long past the time his peers had been toilet trained. He wouldn't wear a diaper most of the day, but when he needed to go, he'd grab one and take it to Kay so she could put it on him. Then he'd do his business and she'd clean him up. We simply couldn't get him to use a toilet.

When we consulted Austin's doctor, he said that one of us would have to lock ourselves in the bathroom with our son and not let him out until he'd used the toilet. Knowing Austin, we knew that might take hours—or days. The misery of that proposition was just too much to contemplate. So we procrastinated.

At the time, Sarah was eight years old and loved to catch frogs. She was a sharp-eyed girl who could spot animals none of the rest of us could see. One day she came home holding a record number—five frogs—in her little hands. Austin was watching as she held one over the toilet. Much to our surprise, that little frog did his business right into the bowl. She told Austin, "See? That's what you're supposed to do."

To Kay's amazement, all this seemed to register with Austin. Perhaps even more impressive was Sarah's apparent telepathic power over frogs.

Not long after that incident, Austin felt nature's call. He fetched a diaper and handed it to Kay, as usual. Exasperated by the routine, Kay was ready with a pair of scissors. Instead of putting the diaper on Austin, she cut it into pieces right in front of him. "That's it," she said. "No more diapers. Use the toilet."

And he did. To this day, both Sarah and Kay give themselves credit for toilet training Austin. Who knows? Maybe it took both of them.

Like other parents of children with autism, we were constantly faced with decisions about how aggressively to deal with our child's disability. First there was the search for a silver-bullet cure. Friends and family sent us countless well-intentioned articles about various therapies and research. Which ones should we pursue? Should we search for a cause? Was autism the result of an allergic reaction? Was it genetic? Would music therapy help? How about vitamin therapy? Some parents choose to devote all their resources to finding an effective course of therapy, often at great cost and sacrifice. They investigate heroically and leave no stone unturned. Thank goodness for them—they are the pathfinders for the rest of us. But we weren't sure we wanted to go that route ourselves.

We knew it would be easy to allow the child who needed the most attention to suck up so much of our energy that there would be none left for the other children. We didn't want our daughters' lives to be dominated by their brother's disability. And we didn't want him to be a cause for resentment.

We could have tried to convince ourselves and the world that Austin was better than other children in some ways. I admit I entertained a few savant fantasies in the early years just after his diagnosis. When Austin remembered the color of each player's miniature golf ball a year after we'd played the game, I hoped he might turn out to have some kind of hidden genius. Although he had a great memory, it seemed to apply only to random things that caught his attention. Not a skill with great marketability. After we saw the movie *Rain Man*, I considered teaching Austin to count cards, thinking he might make a killing in Vegas. He had no interest in the cards or the killing.

In many ways our son was just an ordinary boy with an ordinary family who loved him. We wanted Austin to be cured, but we also wanted him to be integrated into our family. That meant we had to make choices to strike some sort of balance in pursuing both ends. We were determined to help him adjust to this earthling world as effectively as he could. We never felt sure we were doing the right thing or pursuing the best path. That's the thing about autism—it gives you plenty of opportunities to second-guess yourself.

Early in my career, my coworkers came up with an adage about dealing with choices. We called it the Swiss Army Rule: when the map and the terrain differ, go with the terrain.

It seemed as if our lives had been blown off course and we had crash-landed in uncharted territory. We didn't know what lay ahead. It wasn't what we wanted or expected. But we had to press on.

When the map and the terrain differ, go with the terrain.

CHAPTER 3

CONNECTING

SOMETHING WE LEARNED early on with Austin was that it's impossible to raise a child with special needs alone. We were dependent on the assistance and expertise of other people—both professionals and laypeople who cared for us. Many appeared in unexpected ways.

When Austin turned three, he became eligible for special education services. Each morning the "short bus" would arrive at our house, and Kay would strap our toddler into a harness that kept him immobilized and in his seat for the forty-five-minute ride to his school. Sending him on such a long ride, trussed in and alone at such a young age, evoked feelings of guilt for Kay. But it was a godsend for her to have three hours a day to recharge and to focus on our daughters. She looks back on those years with gratitude for the respite.

The bus driver that first year was like an angel sent to help us. Every morning she would arrive at the prearranged time. And then she'd wait because Kay and Austin were never ready. They were inside, battling. Socks. Shoes. Coat. Mittens. Hat. Each item gave Austin cause for struggle and howling resistance. Minute after minute would tick by as the driver waited, engine idling, exhaust billowing into the street. No matter how long the wait was, she never honked.

When mother and son finally emerged, the driver greeted Kay as though nothing were amiss. She showed no impatience. She spoke no words of reproach. The driver's kindness was cool water on a burn, balm for a woman whose wounds were still tender to the touch. Many years later, long after the driver retired, Kay saw her picture in the obituary columns. Although she'd known the driver only as Alice, Kay grieved as though she'd lost a close friend.

When your strength wanes, lean on others to hold you up.

Special education was both a gift and a heartbreak for us. Like other schools around the country, Austin's school was required to develop Individual Educational Plans (IEPs) for students with disabilities and to meet with their parents twice a year. These plans set goals for the students that the schools commit to helping them achieve. The easy chattiness of normal parent-teacher conferences is not for those of us with special-needs children. For us, there are reams of documents and records, multiple teachers and specialists, and dozens of papers to sign. Each time Kay and I went to school for these meetings, sitting with other waiting parents, we were humbled and disheartened all over again, realizing how different our son was from other boys.

Once when I was out of town, Kay attended an IEP meeting alone. The young teacher began by saying, "We've made some progress." Then, under her breath she muttered, "And we've got a long way to go." Kay kept it together until the end of the meeting, but she was in tears by the time she reached her car.

Kay and I were powerless to fix what was wrong with Austin. We needed the talent, skills, and dedication of strangers to help our son. It couldn't have been easy—Austin's teachers ran into a thousand walls trying to get through to him. I tried to compare his education with my own, but the similarities were hard to find. Austin would never write an essay like the one I'd written for my fourth-grade teacher, Mrs. Owens, laying out my plans to go to college, run for office, and eventually become the president of the United States. Such boyish essays—and aspirations—were utterly beyond Austin, and they always would be.

No amount of effort on the part of his parents or teachers would change that.

At the end of each IEP session, I would say to the professionals gathered, "Thank you for all you're doing for our son. What you do here will have much to do with determining the trajectory of his life—perhaps even more than what we do as his parents." I would then walk around the table and shake each person's hand, thanking everyone again. I didn't have control over what happened in the classroom on a daily basis. I simply had to trust. And I wanted them to know that they had my trust. I hoped my vote of confidence would get them through on those days when they wondered if it was worth all the effort.

Other people in our lives tried to understand what we were going through and offered succor in various ways. Once when Austin came up in a casual conversation, an acquaintance from church offered the simplest and most touching gift. She paused, looked me straight in the eye, and said in the kindest voice, "I pray for Austin every day."

Another time, I told our priest that I constantly worried about Austin and wondered if I was up to the task that had been laid out before me. I half expected that he'd tell me to trust in God—a sort of priestly pat on the head—and send me on my way.

Instead, he said, "That's what we're here for. When your strength wanes, lean on others to hold you up."

I'd been thinking that if I wasn't strong all the time, everything would collapse. I also realized that my fears of weakness had been a source of shame. But he was saying that not only was it okay to be weak but it was the natural order of things. Forgiving myself for being weak became the first step of the climb out.

After admitting my weakness to myself, I found it easier to admit it to others, too. More important, by dropping the pretense of invulnerability, I was able to accept their help and gain strength from them. And I became better at lending strength to others.

In the past, I'd never been sure how to act when someone suffered a loss or a failure. I suspected it might be better to simply pretend nothing was wrong. Maybe that was better than saying the wrong thing. But my own pain taught me that it didn't really matter what people said. Intent was what really mattered. The comfort of a kind word or a willing hand was so powerful that it outweighed everything else.

By admitting our weakness, we grow stronger.

CHAPTER 4

FINDING GOLD IN DARK PLACES

Parents with typically abled children tend to have clearly defined victories to celebrate in their children's lives—distinct milestones that mark the passage from one life phase to another. Getting a driver's license. Graduating from high school or college. Getting a first job. Getting married. But for parents who have children with disabilities, the victories can be subtler, harder to notice. We have to be intentional about keeping our eyes open so we don't miss them.

For twelve years Kay stood in the heat and the snow and the rain waving good-bye to the school bus. Austin waved back only once. Our son has never spontaneously said he loves us. That doesn't mean he doesn't—he just communicates love in a different way.

The first time we left Austin and his sisters for any length of time was the winter Kay and I spent a week in Colorado. We returned to find Austin standing on the snowy corner alone, waiting for us. He didn't embrace us. He didn't say he'd missed us. He said, "You were gone a long time."

One wave in twelve years. One boy standing in the snow. Austin has taught us to celebrate the little victories. He has also taught us patience.

We spent years showing Austin how to tie his shoes. It took him so long to learn that we sometimes wondered if he would be a grown man still fastening his shoes with Velcro. But eventually, when he was about nine years old, he conquered his battle with shoelaces.

Patience was needed for haircuts, too, as each one was a fight. I would wrestle Austin to the floor like a steer, scissors in my hand, and cut while we had him pinned. I'm not a great barber, and I knew this method wouldn't work forever. He was going to get bigger, and I was only going to get older and slower.

So we began the long process of teaching Austin to let a barber cut his hair. At first he just sat in the chair. Then the barber held the scissors near his hair and pretended to cut. Next he actually cut off a bit of hair. Each step took months, and it was a full year before Austin would allow the barber to use clippers on him. That was a big day—a huge triumph.

Other small victories came gradually as Austin taught us new ways to communicate with him. If I was frustrated and fussing at him, Austin wasn't able to offer excuses or explanations to assuage my anger, like other children might. But he came up with a strategy all his own. Whenever he saw my furrowed brow, he would run to me and frantically push up my eyebrows, as if they were the cause of the problem. His little hands banished my anger better than any words could have.

As Austin revealed himself to us ever so slowly, always on his own timetable, he taught us that we should never give up on him, never count him out, never think we had him completely figured out.

Shortly after Austin's diagnosis, we were connected with an angel in the guise of Phyllis Kupperman, who became not only his speech therapist but also his cheerleader. For the first seven years of therapy, Austin seemed to ignore everything she tried and continued to play in his own world. But Phyllis never gave up. She kept looking for ways to unlock what was inside him. Austin was nine before he began to regain some of the language he'd lost as a toddler. And even then, he was able to repeat only what had been said to him.

> **Our son has never spontaneously said he loves us. That doesn't mean he doesn't—he just communicates love in a different way.**

Still, there were occasional breakthroughs, even if these moments weren't heralded with trumpets. During one session, Austin was playing with alphabet tiles. To Kay's amazement, Austin began separating all the capital letters from the lowercase letters, although he'd never spoken the letters, identified them, or given any indication that he knew what letters were.

As words slowly came back to Austin, we saw his uniqueness and shared his wonder at interpreting the earthling world. At first his only speech was to echo back the last couple of words he'd just heard. Later he started saying one- or two-word phrases of his own, like "Eyebrows up!" which saved him from having to run across the room to push up my glowering brows. *Chocolate* was the word he used to describe all the things he liked. *Chop* was what he said in reference to things he didn't like.

He began to create new combinations of words to describe things, which we referred to as "Austinisms." "Orange spring" for fall. "Sky flowers" for fireworks. "Walking rock" for turtle. Others were more self-explanatory, such as "bottom sneeze."

Austin still giggles during the sad parts of movies and chuckles at on-screen violence because these scenes don't seem real to him. But my son has the most tender heart of anyone in our family. The day we found an abandoned kitten, he cried all night because its family had left it.

It's not just Austin we've learned about in the two decades he's been with our family; we've also learned a lot about ourselves. Most typically abled kids know to avoid their parents when they're in a bad mood. Instead of avoiding me, Austin will ask me why I'm in a bad mood. His question usually snaps me out of a bad mood by reminding me that my irritation is affecting other people.

Whenever I get angry with Austin, he is unhappy for so long that it breaks my heart. Sometimes he comes to me long after my anger has dissipated to ask why I was mad; other times he shuts down and blames himself. No amount of assurance is enough to soothe him. The pain of watching his suffering has taught me to control my negative impulses more effectively than anything else could have. It has made me realize how much I let trivial things get to me. It has also reminded me that I've snapped at my daughters, too, and that my anger has the same shaming effect on them. The only difference is that they are better at hiding it.

Austin has also taught us to give up any pretensions we might have had about being cool or quietly fitting in. If we enter an elevator with someone of another race, he will announce to the crowd at large, "Everyone is equal." I don't know why he says this. The first time he did so, I tried ignoring him. He said it again—louder this time—which taught me to quickly agree. "Yes, Austin. That's true." I hoped my response would assuage Austin and satisfy the occasional hard stares from others on the elevator. Austin's inability to know what's appropriate and what's not has taught me to go with the flow. You have to go with it, or you go crazy.

Having Austin in our lives has shown us who our true friends are and encouraged us to go deep with them. We've found many true friends in our local church community, where people know our struggle and don't judge us. Or if they do judge us, they have enough judgment not to say anything that gets back to us. Austin has become something of a mascot for St. Michael's Episcopal Church in Barrington as he wanders around the building. Sometimes he strays outside to the graveyard across the street during the service and then comes in sometime during Communion. He walks up to the rail, gets the bread, and eats it as he takes off for who knows where. He's in a safe place, among friends. And so are we.

Look deeper, even into troubles. There is gold to be found everywhere.

CHAPTER 5

BE READY

WHEN AUSTIN WAS four years old, I got a surprise invitation to breakfast with the head of human resources from Walgreens. It was Valentine's Day, 1992. By then I was a partner at my firm, Ernst & Young—a position I'd pursued with singular focus for the past several years. But to my surprise, it was still just a job. The job was fine, but I found myself asking with some disappointment, "Is this what I've been working for all this time?"

This feeling hit home during a partner meeting when the managing partner, talking about our need to reduce costs, said we had too much capacity. I turned to a fellow partner and said, "By capacity, he means us." Excess capacity was not exactly what I'd worked my entire life hoping to be.

That Valentine's Day marked five years of on-site consulting with Walgreens, working on IT systems for their distribution centers and inventory management. I was about to move back to the Ernst & Young office in downtown Chicago when Walgreens offered me a permanent position. The human resources head said

I would be a good fit with their company, partly because they believed I could relate well with all levels of the division, including those on the floor where the work gets done. I took this as the highest of compliments. My parents, who had spent their lives on the floor where the work gets done, would have been proud.

When Kay and I had moved to an affluent suburb of Chicago several years before, my dad often said that I didn't live in the real America. Maybe not. But I hadn't forgotten where I came from. I was raised in Wichita Falls, Texas, where the lessons of the Great Depression hadn't been forgotten, where people regularly worried about losing their jobs and whether they'd be able to put food on the table, where people took jobs not because they felt some calling but because they needed the money.

> **I would rather have someone worry about disappointing me than be afraid of me.**

In family pictures from my childhood, I'm usually wearing jeans held up by both a belt and suspenders. We bought the pants long so I could grow into them. Mom sewed patches on the inside of the knees so the holes wouldn't show as they wore down. We drove a Nash Rambler, referred to as the "Thinking Man's Car"—probably because it was too ugly to be the sexy man's car.

My father, like his father and grandfather before him, was a railroad man. He had signed on with the railroad right out of high school, and not long after, he married my mom. A couple of years later he was drafted and sent to the war in Germany.

Dad never said much to me directly. I learned about his attitudes and opinions mostly from listening to him and his friends talk about work. He didn't care much for bosses who didn't understand or appreciate how work gets done. In one rare direct exchange, he told me that if I ever had anybody work for me, it would be better if they worried about disappointing me than if they were afraid of me. It turned out to be good advice.

The job offer from Walgreens had come completely out of the blue. I'd never considered working there before, nor had anyone implied the company was interested in me. But in an instant, I knew this was the right fit. This was a successful, old-line company, steeped in tradition and deep values. It had a promote-from-within philosophy with low turnover in the executive offices, and it was positioned perfectly for growth and new opportunities. Walgreens was the leader in logistics and wanted to stay that way. The job was everything I'd been preparing for my whole career—a place where I could use all the skills I'd developed in seventeen years as a consultant. And one more thing: they knew me and they wanted me. I took a cut in pay to accept the offer.

I wanted to do great things. I wanted to build something big. I was looking for great success, great achievement, a great future. I had found my home.

You're being prepared for something even if you don't know what it is. Be ready.

CHAPTER 6

ARCHIMEDES AND THE SCORPION

MOST EVERYONE COMES to a new job with enthusiasm and great expectations. When I joined Walgreens, I was ready to set the world on fire. Not everyone was convinced I would, however. When a Walgreens analyst on the project I had led as a consultant learned I'd been offered the job, she asked me why Walgreens had picked me.

"Maybe because I bring some different skills and experience," I replied.

She still looked skeptical. As the air rushed out of my swollen head, I offered her a smile. "Or maybe they don't know me as well as you do." She seemed more satisfied with that answer.

If she was skeptical because she thought I'd have to run pretty fast to make my experience match the challenges ahead, she wasn't far off.

In the past I'd managed consultants, who tend to be smart, well educated, and self-motivated. The key to managing a team of consultants is to show them what success looks like and then get out of the way. Getting from point A to B is usually a pretty straight line.

On the other hand, leading a division with thousands of employees and operations spread across the country meant there were few straight lines to follow. The job was not only to achieve current objectives but also to be prepared to meet whatever future challenges the company might face. I needed to take a step back for some self-examination to determine what my values were. What kind of boss did I want to be?

Archimedes, the Greek father of math, said "Give me a place to stand and with a lever I will move the whole world." As we go through life, we seek ways to influence the world around us. Our skills, determination, and talents are the levers. Knowing who we are and the principles we cling to, called "first principles," forms the foundation for our actions—the values we fall back on in times of trouble or uncertainty.

One of my early first principles was my mom's constant reminder, "You're as good as anybody." She was raised dirt-poor on a tenant farm during the Depression. She didn't want her children bridled with shame because of who they were or where they came from. This first principle helped me develop both high self-esteem and poor judgment in knowing when to keep my mouth shut.

One of my most important first principles was revealed during a time of trouble a few years earlier. Our first child, Sarah, was not quite a year old when she contracted a form of meningitis that is often fatal. As she lay in intensive care, the doctors assured us they were doing all they could. But they wouldn't tell us that everything was going to be all right.

I don't think there is a love stronger than a parent's love for his or her child. The saying that there are no atheists in foxholes goes for parents in ICU waiting rooms at children's hospitals as well. At that point all Kay and I had was each other and prayer.

At a church series earlier that year, I'd learned a meditative technique for study and prayer in which we took a Bible reading and pretended we were in it. The priest said that as we quieted our minds, the story might take on a life of its own, much the way a dream does at the edge of sleep. That week's verse was one in which Jesus is asked who he is and he responds with a parable.

So as we all closed our eyes and the room settled into silence, I imagined myself in the crowd gathered around Jesus. I took solace in the fact that the apostles

> **"Give me a place to stand and with a lever I will move the whole world."**
>
> —ARCHIMEDES

probably didn't understeand the parable either. In a moment of exasperation, I said to Jesus, "Why are you always beating around the bush with these parables and this Son of Man stuff? Why don't you come out and be clear? Are you really God?"

He turned and said, "Would you believe me if I told you?"

Hmm. That was unexpected. And right on target. *Would I?* I wondered. Maybe not. Then I asked, "How will I know, then?"

"You will know that I am real by the changes I make in others. You will see me in other people's lives." I hadn't seen that coming.

Afterward, when the priest asked for comments, my hand shot into the air. For me the exchange offered insight not only about the verse but also about an important aspect of faith. Later the priest suggested we try the same technique when praying for others by imagining ourselves taking them to Jesus.

Now, several months later, as I sat watching over Sarah in the hospital bed late at night, that time had come. With Kay asleep in the chair beside me, I closed my eyes and imagined that Kay and I were carrying Sarah in our arms up a grassy hill to a bench, where Jesus sat with his back to us.

When he turned around, we said, "This is our daughter, Sarah. Please heal her. She is sick, and we love her so."

Without a word, he took her in his arms and started walking away. Kay and I became very upset, pleading with him not to take her. He looked back and asked, "Why are you so sad? She is going to be with me. All her pain will be gone. And her head won't hurt anymore. She will be with me forever and know nothing but joy."

I knew then that my distress stemmed from my own selfishness. Our plans and hopes were being dashed. "You're right," I said. "We are crying for ourselves."

Jesus then stretched out his arms and gave her back to us. Silently he walked away.

Just as in so many Bible stories, Jesus had done something obviously profound. And equally ambiguous. Did this mean she would be healed? I wasn't sure. I hoped so. But one thing was certain about his message: the source of my pain was my selfish fear of loss. Having confronted that fact gave me a degree of peace and helped me not to be paralyzed by the terrible what-ifs that were playing out in my head.

A few days later, the lab results came in, and Sarah was switched to a more effective antibiotic to fight the infection. She gradually improved, and after a month in the hospital, we rejoiced when we were finally able to take her home. We were aware, however, that for many other parents in the ICU, there would only be tears of sorrow.

I have often recalled that experience over the years, from the perspective of both a parent and a boss. In that waiting room, all of us from different backgrounds felt the same way about our children. There was no rich or poor, no distinctions between race or creed. On one side of the glass were parents who loved so intensely we would be willing to make any sacrifice for our children, and on the other side were those worthy of such love.

As these children grew up, how could anyone disregard or abuse these precious sons and daughters? How could any boss regard them as if they were just interchangeable parts in a machine or as merely a means to an end?

I realized that this kind of love doesn't happen just in hospitals. With this knowledge, how could I treat those around me as any less than I hoped they would treat the ones I love?

Sometimes a first principle is formed by circumstances, as it was with Sarah. Other times it's revealed through grappling with a hard choice, as it was with a conflict over my baptism. For generations, all my family members were stalwarts in a Protestant denomination that prides itself on strict adherence to the Bible. Drinking and dancing were not allowed. Although musical instruments were forbidden in church, there was excellent singing in four-part harmony to compensate for the lack of accompaniment. Traditionally, members were baptized during their teen years in the permanent baptismal pool behind the pulpit. Many a Sunday I saw young people and adults in their white robes wading into the water to be submersed. After an internal dispute, we left the church during my teen years, and I never got baptized.

In my twenties, I found my way back to church as an Episcopalian, where I was baptized by the bishop, who poured water over my head. This did not sit well with my family, who didn't believe that getting my head wet was an effective alternative to complete immersion. My grandmother went to her grave convinced that I was going to hell, and I knew my parents were concerned too.

When I sought my priest's advice, he suggested I tell them that my Episcopal baptism was perfectly sufficient and not to worry. Although I agreed my baptism was valid, I knew this line of reasoning would have gone over like a lead balloon. I wanted to do the right thing. And what was the right thing, the unselfish thing? I fell back on the beautiful Bible verses heard at almost every Christian wedding, which describe love as being patient and kind, not arrogant or rude, not insisting on its own way. The verses end with the statement that of the three things that will last forever— faith, hope, and love—love is the greatest.

So finally, on a visit back to Texas, I offered to let Dad baptize me. With Kay and Mom standing on the edge of my parents' swimming pool, Dad and I waded out into the middle. Just as he was ready to begin, Dad asked me if this meant I was renouncing my Episcopal baptism. I considered and then replied, "No. It's up to God to figure out those kinds of things. I know that I am called to be a loving son."

Dad nodded and we proceeded. From that moment, I realized that one of the first principles of my faith is love. I may not always act accordingly, but I know what the standard is and what to cling to when there is a choice to be made.

Without first principles, it's easy to be tossed about by the circumstances of the day like a cork in a storm. But while first principles anchor us, they aren't much different from aspirations until they're tested. There's a traditional Hindu story about a master and a student that demonstrates the difference. The two are crossing a river, and about halfway across, the master notices a scorpion floating in the water alongside him. Rather than let it drown, he reaches down and gently scoops it out of the water. Immediately the scorpion stings him. But the master continues wading. Before he reaches the other side, the scorpion stings him again, bringing him to his knees. He continues on and finally reaches the shore, where he lowers the scorpion safely to the ground.

The student is incredulous. "Why did you pick it up knowing it would likely sting you? And why did you keep going once it did?"

The master replies, "It's the scorpion's nature to sting me. It is my nature to save it. Why should I let his nature define mine?"

Cling to your principles. They will give you courage to do the right thing, especially when it's the hardest thing.

CHAPTER 7

MONEY, MISSION, AND MEANING

BUSINESS HAS FIRST principles too. I'm happy to say that aligning business principles with my own first principles hasn't been as difficult as some people led me to believe it would be.

In business school, a primary lesson that was drilled into me was that a business must take care of its owners above all others. When Nobel economist Milton Friedman visited our campus in Austin, he took that lesson to the extreme, telling us that companies should eschew charitable works in favor of maximizing shareholders' wealth. The shareholders could then choose how to spend their earnings. Some executives agree, which makes it easy for them to resolve conflicts when the interests of shareholders seem to be in conflict with other values. But I didn't find it so easy to agree.

I had even more trouble agreeing when my favorite economics professor said that if it weren't against the law, a business should remove its trash by throwing it in the nearest river. He meant that this was the smart economic answer. But does business have no responsibility to the community it serves? Is *ethical* to be defined as "whatever is legal"?

. There seemed to be some conflict between the first principles of the businesses those two professors were talking about and the first principles I held most dear. How could a guy who had participated in the first Earth Day celebration throw trash in a river? As a young man, I had inscribed one of John Donne's famous poems in my journal. It begins, "No man is an island, entire of itself."

As a student, I found these conflicting views to be interesting philosophical questions, but as my power and responsibility in the business world grew, such conundrums became more real and held higher stakes for me. I decided early on that while we should never lose sight of the shareholders' interests or stray from our fiduciary duties, we need to keep in mind that we are also stewards of power that impacts employees and the community at large. Power carries an awesome responsibility.

Meaning is why we climb.

Fortunately, in practice, much of the business community sees itself as serving not only shareholders but also other stakeholders, such as customers, the community, and employees, who are directly affected by its actions.

Knowing my first principles helped me keep myself grounded in the corporate world. Careerism, greed, and other types of self-serving behavior are present in every company, as they are in all of life. But I've found that taking the high road is always the best route to any destination. You get where you want to go just as quickly—plus the view is a lot better.

In my job as head of a new department formed by long-time employees, I would have to prove myself and work to find common ground. One way of doing that was to agree about the work before us—what we needed to do and how we should go about doing it.

From my consulting days, I had learned that people are motivated by the following factors, in ascending sequence of effectiveness: money, mission, and meaning. It's no surprise that money is important up to a certain point, but for most people, mission and meaning are more effective in bringing out the best in us.

Mission, which is where most businesses concentrate their motivational efforts, is about achievement. It's about productive action that is focused on a clearly stated goal. People do great things for a worthy mission, and much satisfaction can be found in such achievement. It inspires people to use their talents, challenges them to work hard, and gives them a sense of pride in what they've accomplished.

We needed to define our mission and set about developing a mission statement—a task that's usually approached with dread by anyone assigned the task. To prevent our statement from being one of those trite, generic slogans that put me to sleep before I reach the end of the sentence, I invited the team to craft and examine each word of our mission statement.

Here's what we came up with: "Our mission is the never-ending pursuit of better ways to manage the flow of merchandise from our suppliers to our customers." Straightforward. Clear. And perhaps a bit trite and generic. But then we fleshed out a paragraph for each key word or phrase of the statement—*never-ending pursuit, better, ways, manage, flow, suppliers, customers*—to explain what each meant in the context of our work and attitudes, and why each was important. When we did so, our statement no longer felt trite and generic. It represented our view of what was important and how we hoped to achieve our vision. It described us at our best. We started each meeting by having various team members read respective parts of the mission statement aloud. Hearing the words spoken aloud made them come alive, gave them power, and reminded us of who we aspired to be.

Our mission statement covered the essentials. It was the lodestone that would keep us close to our essential purpose. Our mission clarified what and how. Mission gets us to the top of the mountain. But it doesn't tell us why we do it. Meaning is why we climb.

All of us want to believe our work is worthy of our efforts. Meaning provides the answer. In his well-known book *Man's Search for Meaning*, concentration camp survivor Viktor Frankl observes that we can endure any *what* if we have a *why*.

During the civil rights movement in the 1960s, my family's black-and-white TV showed unarmed civil rights protesters risking their lives as they faced fire hoses, nightsticks, and dogs. They didn't know whether their efforts would be successful, but they knew their cause was worth the risk and the sacrifice. It isn't a guarantee of success that spurs us to greatness; it's knowing that we're working for something greater than ourselves.

At Walgreens we started looking at the meaning of our work by defining who we were doing all this work for. I came up with a way to remember the groups of stakeholders we were beholden to: customers, employees, shareholders, and society. I called it the CESSpool of stakeholders. Crude, but memorable.

My professors' intellectual discussions about the ultimate importance of shareholders once again failed to carry much water in the real world when it came time to motivate the people who actually did the work. Taking care of customers, ensuring fellow employees a satisfying work environment, and bettering the community topped shareholders every time. Since we worked for a drugstore chain, it wasn't difficult to find meaning in a business where what you do for customers can literally mean the difference between life and death.

Knowing the importance of meaning, I wanted to take every opportunity to help our people understand how important their work was. When I was given responsibility for the entire division a few years later, I visited every distribution center and conducted town hall meetings and question-and-answer sessions with all four thousand employees across every shift. In each of the sixty-five sessions I conducted during my first six months on the job, I ended by reading a letter from a customer whose daughter had cancer. The mother wrote that one day she had discovered she was out of her daughter's medicine. She called the store in a panic, only to learn that the pharmacy had already closed. The store manager said, "It's not a problem." The manager called the pharmacist at home, and by the time the mother had arrived at the store, the medicine was waiting for her. Perhaps the store manager could have referred the mother to a twenty-four-hour pharmacy across town, but she didn't, because that mother and that child were her customers. Not somebody else's.

> **It isn't a guarantee of success that spurs us to greatness; it's knowing that we're working for something greater than ourselves.**

I read that letter sixty-five times, because when you're standing there on a concrete floor hour after hour, packing cases, you're a long way from the people you're serving. I wanted them to know that their work had meaning. I wanted them to know that they were part of something larger. And the story of the girl with cancer wasn't just the manager's story. It was their story too.

If work is only about mission, only the end matters. If it has meaning, every day matters.

CHAPTER 8

PRINCIPLES
REQUIRE ACTION

THE IDEA THAT much is expected of those who have been given much had been drilled into me as a boy. I saw giving back as my duty—a responsibility I'd accepted from a young age. Feeling the duty to help others after graduating from college, I signed up for the Peace Corps and served two years in a small Peruvian village.

I arrived at my village at age twenty-one filled with nobility, pumped up with the idea of helping humankind. I was proud that I had something to offer these poor folks. But one day, after I'd finally learned enough Spanish to communicate, one of the farmers asked me a question that must have been on everyone's mind but mine.

"Why did they send you?" he asked. "If they wanted to help us, why didn't they send a tractor?"

I don't remember my answer, but I never forgot his question. I'll never know if I did the Peruvians any good, but they taught me a lot—how much we are alike, that wealth is relative, that a good time can be had under any circumstances, and that no one is too old to dance. And based on their ingenuity, which I witnessed over and over again, I know they would have figured out a way to keep that tractor running long after I returned to the United States.

Many businesses feel the same pull of duty I did when it comes to helping the community. Charitable support is the way businesses most often try to connect. After all, businesses are the haves; the needy are the have-nots. Charity may represent only a small dent in corporate culture, but it pays off in big ways. For one thing, the company benefits from the goodwill generated in the community and among employees. Traditionally, many executives participate in charitable events, volunteer for committees, and serve on boards. But I didn't engage in a lot of those activities. I was busy doing my job and handling my home life. With the challenges of three small children, including one with special needs, and the closest family member five hundred miles away, Kay needed all the support she could get.

That didn't mean I wasn't feeling the call to get involved. I often lay in bed at night, feeling completely helpless and alone, just as millions of other parents do, hearing the old clock ticking off the days of my life and worrying about leaving behind a child who wouldn't be able to care for himself. Endless questions haunted me. *How can I ever save enough to ensure that our child won't end up on the streets after we're gone? Will he be safe? Who will worry about him? Who will care for him?* I know all parents with a child with disabilities share the same prayer: to live one day longer than our child. And I know its corollary for every child: that our child will live to his potential in safety and health. Every time Kay and I went into Austin's classroom, we came out grieving over not just Austin but all the kids there. What would happen to them? Having children of my own has taught me about the fierce, unflagging love of parents. Having a child with a disability has taught me about those parents' unique pain.

Charity is a good start, but it isn't a game changer. Just like I wasn't the tractor the Peruvian farmers had needed. Charity wasn't what people like my son really needed; they needed jobs. Only a job could give them a place in this world. As long as they were dependent on others, they would be considered second-class citizens. With a paying job, however, they would be part of our world—not relegated to the shadows and reliant on the charity of strangers. Work would fill their days, offer healthy challenges, and provide relationships. Work would mean independence.

And here I was, in charge of a growing division that hired more than six hundred entry-level employees a year. Soon that number would grow to more than a

Charity is a good start, but it isn't a game changer.

thousand annually. I started to think of the lives we could impact, and it began to gnaw at me. I didn't have a plan, but I knew the problem. And I knew that Walgreens had something that was desperately needed: jobs.

Based on my upbringing and experience, I believed it my duty to go beyond my own self-interests to positively impact the world around me. But it wasn't enough to believe it; I needed to act on that belief. The power of any principle lies in the action it inspires. In other words, the *why* is useless without the *what*. And the what is more difficult. As Alfred Adler observed, it is easier to fight for one's principles than it is to live up to them.

Gradually the task I needed to accomplish came into focus. The community had once been merely a token placeholder on the stakeholder map. My business professors had assumed that serving shareholders and society was an either-or decision. But they were wrong. It was becoming clear to me that this was a both-and decision. We had jobs. People with disabilities needed jobs. If we looked at people as resources instead of merely recipients of charity, we could serve both their needs and ours. We would have to be more creative than we'd been in the past. But was it worth the effort? Absolutely. Were we up to it? I certainly hoped so.

The power of any principle lies in the action it inspires.

It wasn't going to be a choice between the community and shareholders. We could serve both. It wasn't a choice between mission and meaning, between achieving our business goals and making a difference in the community. We could do both. And it wasn't a choice between being excellent and employing people with disabilities. We could do both.

We would do both.

Principles are only the starting point. If you want to make a difference in the world, you need to act on what you believe.

CHAPTER 9

FIND THE CRACK IN
THE CONCRETE

WALGREENS COULD BE an old-fashioned kind of place in some ways. Case in point: people were still referring to supervisors as "Mr.," "Mrs.," and "Ms." long after using such titles was a thing of the past at other companies. At my first officer meeting the day after I was promoted to vice president, President Dan Jorndt, a whirling dervish of energy who always bounded up the steps two at a time, had invited me to stop by his office. He said that he was delighted to have me and that he thought I would do great things at Walgreens. He told me that part of my legendary predecessor's success was due to the fact that he'd given the credit to those below him. He advised me to do the same.

Feeling pretty good as I stood up to leave, I decided to take the opportunity to address this "Mister" thing, which I thought was unnecessary. I turned and said as offhandedly as possible, "You know, I never had a boss that I called Mister." Mr. Jorndt had already begun reading something on his desk, and there was a short pause before he looked up. With a slight smile, he said, "Well, you do now."

I nodded. This was a serious place indeed!

And like all businesses, Walgreens was serious about making money. They did so effectively, too. Over the next decade, the company solidified its position as the largest drugstore chain in America. I'm proud to have been a part of that.

Walgreens is a member of the Fortune 50. It's a publicly traded company, which means it's competitive. It's about business. But it isn't all about business—no company is. That's because companies are filled with people. Anywhere you have people, you'll also find the desire to do good. That doesn't mean everybody, all the time. People and businesses may do wrong in all sorts of ways. They act selfishly; they take the easy way out. And yet, if they get the chance—if they're able to see a way that won't cost them more than they can afford—they'll often jump out there and do what's right. The desire for a meaningful life is always present in people—strong and silent, just waiting for its chance. All that desire needs is an outlet, a crack in the concrete that will allow it to bloom.

In the kind of coincidence that hindsight indicates is ordained, Walgreens already had some cracks in the concrete that seemed custom ordered for me. One of the most familiar photographs in the history of Walgreens is more than one hundred years old. The photo is of two employees, one African American and the other white, standing in front of the first Walgreens store. No one knows who the white man is, but the black man, Silas Danner, is probably the most well-known employee from the early days of Walgreens. According to store history, when someone called with an order, Charles Walgreen would keep the customer on the phone long enough for Silas to assemble the order and then run to the customer's house. The customer would have to excuse himself or herself from the call to answer the door, where Silas was waiting with the purchase.

Silas's contribution to the company was not an exception. The Walgreens commitment to fairness arises from a long-standing tradition of equality. Charles R. Walgreen, the company's founder, employed African American pharmacists starting in the early 1900s, when he was just beginning his business, and paid them the same wages he paid white pharmacists—something that was unheard of in those days.

Anywhere you have people, you'll also find the desire to do good.

As the following letter from Mr. Walgreen to one of his store managers shows, not everyone in the company wanted to go along with this policy of equality, but Mr. Walgreen would not back down.

Daytona Beach, Florida
April 4, 1928

Dear Mr. Wilkinson,

Returned to Seabreeze last evening—found several letters among which was one from Mrs. Bakerhill (Mattie) who said Mr. B. was having some trouble about his salary. Possibly you will recall that when he was in the office he stated he had been receiving $45.06 per week and I told him we would pay $50.00 which is our regular price for

Registered Pharmacists and will you please see that he is paid this amount and reimbursed to date.

I have a very definite reason for paying colored R.P.s the same as white and I regret very much that my wishes were not carried out, but please have the matter rectified at once.

I will probably not return for a couple of weeks yet.

Yours,
CRW

Although the Walgreens commitment to equality and justice hadn't yet been directed toward people with disabilities, I took comfort in knowing my company had a good track record—a history of doing the right thing and making money at the same time. If I ever wanted to do something for people with disabilities, I wouldn't have to persuade people who had never considered that justice and equality might be part of their corporate mandate. The company was already there—I'd have only to remind them.

The desire to do good is always there. All you need to do is find a crack in the concrete for it to come through.

CHAPTER 10

PLAYING CHESS

During Dan Jorndt's tenure as CEO, he frequently talked about an incremental strategy for innovation: crawl, walk, run. *Crawl:* start small to become comfortable that the new idea will work. *Walk:* build the idea out enough to know that it could be scaled to the size we need. And then *run* like the wind with it.

It was 1998, six years after I'd signed on with Walgreens. My basic idea was to integrate people with disabilities into our operations. The easiest way to start—the crawling part—was to use something called work-study—a disability jobs program that was already in place in school systems across the country.

I was in charge of the Walgreens transportation and distribution centers, or DCs. So I started there. For the first time, we included all two hundred of the frontline supervisors in addition to the higher-level managers at the annual operations conference that year. In my closing speech, I told them about Austin. He was ten then—a long way from being ready for the work-study jobs that the special-education programs line up for students with disabilities, but I had a pretty good idea of what lay ahead for him in the future. I told the managers about students in special-education classes across the country who struggled to find jobs. I said they needed a chance, and we could give them one. It was a rousing speech. I felt great about it.

The structure for hiring and supervising students in work-study programs was already in place. Now that the mangers knew about the need and a possible solution, I just assumed they would sign on. The schools would send us students with disabilities. The students would get experience that would set them up for future employment. Simple. A no-brainer. Everybody wants to do good, right?

Then nothing much happened.

I had forgotten a lesson I'd learned in the Peace Corps while playing chess with a Peruvian man who always beat me. After countless games, I began to improve, but I still couldn't win. One day he made a keen observation: "I notice that you're planning each of your

You may be planning each of your moves more carefully, but don't forget one key thing: there are two people playing the game.

moves more carefully, but you have forgotten one key thing: there are two people playing the game."

I'd been so focused on what I most wanted to do that I'd forgotten what the managers and supervisors wanted. What they wanted to do—what they had to do—was move product. I'd touched their hearts, but the world is a practical place with lots of practical things that need to get done. It's also a place with lots of sad stories. The story of kids with disabilities was just one more.

Sure, the managers and supervisors wanted to please me. But we had no specific goals and no timetable. I'd acquainted the managers with a problem, but it wasn't their problem. Most important,

I hadn't showed them how what I wanted to do would help them do what they wanted to do.

It was a beginner's mistake.

To enlarge the mission, enlarge the vision.

CHAPTER 11

FAILURE IS JUST
A TIME-OUT

Work-study wasn't the answer I'd been hoping for. Out of the twelve DCs that started a program, only five experienced success. Each facility employed only five or six students, and all of them were successful, high-functioning individuals. None had a disability as severe as Austin's. Why? The work-study teachers wanted their students to succeed. So they sent us the ones they knew could fit in and do the work. Perfectly understandable. Practical—maybe even wise. But we wanted to dig deeper. We wanted students who wouldn't get a chance anywhere else.

The other seven work-study programs never got off the ground. They were hamstrung by the very schools they were trying to help. Some school districts asked for more in return than our distribution centers could provide. Some wanted the DCs to pay the kids a salary, but we didn't have the budget for that. Some wanted the DCs to provide transportation. We didn't have funds for that, either. Even more crippling was the fact that every school district had a bag of expectations and its own rules. Over time we might have made it work, but with our limited resources, it quickly became clear that we needed to admit failure.

Nobody likes failure. But the biggest danger in life—and in business—isn't failure. It's pretending that failure is the exception instead of what it really is: merely part of the process.

I saw a demonstration of this principle one afternoon in Central Park when I came across a small area where people were throwing a Frisbee. They were doing all kinds of throws—overhanded, underhanded, over their shoulders—and making catches with such grace that it almost made me ache with envy. I sat down to watch. Instead of standing across the field from each other, as I usually saw people doing, they were standing about twenty feet apart.

As I watched, I noticed that they missed their catches a lot more often than not—success was the exception in this case. But their attempts were spectacular. And they never gave up. I found myself focusing on certain individuals who would fail again and again at the same trick, and then I'd silently cheer when they got it right. What had appeared effortless and perfect was something else altogether. It reminded me that whenever I see a flawless performance, my applause should be for the unseen hours of commitment, the failures, and the perseverance.

As I continued to watch, I thought about my own experience with skiing. I'd skied for years, but I'd never gotten one bit better. I had no idea why. Now I saw that it was because I'd tried so hard to avoid falling down. Falling is inconvenient. It's embarrassing. And sometimes it hurts. But if I'm not trying hard enough to risk falling, I am not trying hard enough to get better.

Some failures in real life are merely tumbles, but others are more like being caught in an avalanche. I knew that firsthand.

But each time I've failed, I've found that failure is a teacher. It's a fitness center for the soul. Success is constantly kissing up to us, telling us how great we are. Failure, in contrast, knocks us flat on our backs and says, "Welcome to the Big Time." Failure brings us back into the present moment as we catch our breath and brush ourselves off. It gives us pause to figure out what happened and what's next. Time

> **If I'm not trying hard enough to risk falling, I am not trying hard enough to get better.**

spent blaming the conditions or ourselves is better spent deciding whether it's time to look for a way out or make an adjustment and keep going.

As we looked back on the work-study initiative, it was clear that we didn't have the resources or the amount of effort needed to make it a success. It was time to look for another way.

The willingness to fail is the first step toward success.

CHAPTER 12

COMPASSION AND JUSTICE

AFTER OUR FLOPPED work-study experiment, we turned our attention to enclaves. Enclaves consist of contracted workers who are recruited, managed, and paid by a sponsoring organization such as Goodwill. Tasks are usually simple, even tedious. Some employers have enclave workers do cleanup or simple sorting tasks. For example, in a distribution setting, enclave workers might attach security tags to expensive products.

Once again, we had successes and failures. The DC in Jupiter, Florida, looked like it was going well until we realized we were paying the local Goodwill more per worker in the enclave than we were paying our own employees. That wasn't fair to our team members or our shareholders. However, our DC in Wisconsin seemed to have things together—high production, reasonable costs.

And the enclave in Perrysburg, Ohio, was working out exactly as I'd hoped it would. Located on the edge of Toledo in a highly industrialized, unionized area that had suffered a number of job losses, the Perrysburg DC had just recently opened. The manager there was a cool, self-assured man named Keith Scarbrough, whom we'd brought in from the outside. We usually promote managers from within, but Keith impressed me right away as the kind of guy who could sit in the cockpit during a tornado while assuring the passengers in a calm, confident voice that everything was under control and all would be fine. He never let anybody see him sweat.

Maybe one of the reasons Keith put so much effort into making the enclave work was that he knew well what it was like to start at the bottom. Keith grew up in a little Arkansas town called Searcy, where he got his first job sacking groceries. After spending a summer picking strawberries and cucumbers, he worked his way into management at Walmart.

I knew from family lore and from my own experiences that people who work the fields know how to work hard. My grandmother and my mother had told me enough stories about chopping, picking, and pulling cotton that I knew the different processes for each. And I knew to avoid them all.

When I was in high school, I picked cucumbers one summer. That job was no fun—you spend all day bent over looking for cucumbers, you're paid by the pound, and the bosses want you to pick the small ones, not the big ones, which conflicted with my teenage objective of earning the most for the least effort. I lasted three days.

The fact that Keith had made it through an entire summer of picking was a noteworthy achievement. He knew firsthand what hard work was, and he liked the work ethic he saw in the enclave workers.

"There was absolutely zero drama," Keith says. "They came in, did their jobs, and went home, and then they came back the next day." They worked full shifts. They didn't malinger. They didn't become distracted and slow down during the second half of the day.

Keith tells the story of one worker with a disability who found himself without transportation. Instead of calling in, he walked more than an hour to work. Keith had seen what I wanted everyone to see. Having people with disabilities as workers was good business. Making a convert of him would later prove to be a big win.

But first, two things happened in quick succession that forever changed the course of my time at Walgreens. A chance meeting showed me what I truly yearned to create. Then a disappointment hardened my resolve.

The chance meeting happened during a visit to the Waxahachie distribution center outside Dallas, where a team member regaled me with tales of how well the enclave was working, how happy everyone was, and how efficiently everything was operating. I was feeling good. Then she showed me a picture of the enclave members. Everyone was wearing matching T-shirts, and she was standing among them. My face must have registered surprise when I saw the photo. "Oh, I'm not part of the enclave," she said. "I'm one of their sponsors." It was clear that she wanted me to know she wasn't one of them.

For a few blissful moments, I'd thought that people with disabilities were being included in the workforce as a whole. I'd thought they were accepted and valued as part of the operation by team members outside the enclave. But I was wrong. Of course— separate is separate. The individuals with disabilities had jobs, but they weren't part of the workforce. Not really. They weren't *us*; they were still *them*. That's not the kind of world I wanted for my child. I wanted a world where there's no such thing as *them*.

The Waxahachie woman's offhand comment was revealing. It made my heart ache anew for all those who are on the outside looking in.

Not long afterward, an incident with a pizza parlor manager showed me in a personal way how cold the world can be for those on the outside. And it gave me another goad to dream big for those with disabilities.

Austin's high school work-study internship was at a local pizza parlor, where he studied the art of making pizza dough with admirable intensity. His teacher-coach told us that Austin lived for making the dough. And that wasn't all—his coworkers liked him, and so did the customers.

> **Seeing the biases that individuals with disabilities face even from well-intentioned people deepened my compassion and inspired an even greater longing for justice.**

He was endlessly loyal—a cheerful, willing pizza-dough maker. He was never hungover or drugged up. He didn't steal. He didn't gossip or lie. He loved the work. So when his internship was over, we asked the pizza parlor manager if Austin could keep his job making pizza dough. He would work any hours—late nights, weekends, the hours no one else wanted to work.

The manager said, "I don't think so."

"Okay," we said, "what if Austin worked for less money?"

"I don't think so."

"What if Austin had a job coach with him at all times to make sure the work was done correctly?" They would have two employees for less than the price of one.

"I don't think so."

"What if Austin worked the hours no one else wanted, with a job coach, for free?"

"I'm sorry. I don't think so."

No matter what Austin had overcome, no matter what he could do, he was still shut out. And so are countless other individuals like him.

Why wouldn't the manager let him work? We'll never know for sure. I suspect it's because Austin is, in a word, weird. When Austin was first diagnosed and the outlook was dismal, *weird* was a level of achievement we would have been content with. Perhaps it's pejorative to many, but it was better than *unpredictable* or *scary*. I myself have had more than one friend I considered weird, so I thought weird might be enough to win him acceptance. But weird wasn't good enough at the pizza parlor. Weird was enough to keep him out of the game. That and only that. Weird.

Many nights I lay awake in bed, so angry I couldn't sleep. Seeing the biases that individuals with disabilities face even from well-intentioned people deepened my compassion and inspired an even greater longing for justice. My mind wandered back to a consulting engagement when I'd worked for the Dallas transit system. A big issue at the time was that people with disabilities were demanding that lifts be put on city buses. The Transit Authority offered free cab rides to those who were unable to board buses. Lifts would cost more than cabs, and in the eyes of the Transit Authority, the issue was providing transportation at the lowest cost. I now understood why people with disabilities had refused to accept the free cab rides. They wanted accessible buses so they could use public transportation like any other citizen. It was a matter of being included, not just a transportation issue.

My mind flashed back to the image of kids with disabilities crawling up the steps of the US Capitol building during the days before the passage of the Americans with Disabilities Act in 1990. I understood why they'd crawled. They crawled for the same reason sanitation workers wore "I AM A MAN" signs at the 1968 Memphis sanitation strike during the civil rights movement.

When I'd first started trying to help people with disabilities, I was motivated by the sense of duty instilled in me by my upbringing. Later, as we progressed in our experiences with Austin, I moved from duty to compassion. Compassion is a powerful motivator. It literally means "to suffer with." Compassion goes beyond sympathy and pity, allowing us to experience other people's pain to such a degree that we are stirred to relieve it. I felt the pain of other families and was compelled to act. Compassion is not satisfied with the world as it is.

But the pizza parlor incident had shown me that even compassion isn't enough. As long as managers hire people with disabilities as an act of charity, they will never see past the stereotypes that are holding people with disabilities back. Those stereotypes—that individuals with disabilities can't do the work as well, cost more, cause legal suits, have accidents, raise insurance rates, and fail to fit in with the rest of the workforce or the customers—are a wall that no amount of charity will ever overcome. As Saint Augustine observed in the fifth century, "Charity is no substitute for justice withheld."

If we could help dispel those unjust stereotypes, we would be defending against prejudice and exclusion. We wouldn't be offering opportunities to people with disabilities as an act of charity;

instead, we would be promoting the cause of justice. As the idea took shape, my anger was being transformed into resolve.

I wasn't going to burn down any buildings. I wouldn't try to topple the system. I wasn't going to neglect my duties as an officer. To the contrary, my realization reinvigorated me.

I came to see that the problem was not that others were against people with disabilities; the problem was that they avoided them. One reason people with disabilities face so much discrimination is that they often frighten us. We're afraid we might do or say something that will offend them. We're afraid to feel the pity that might arise within us. We're afraid of the vulnerability it exposes about our own humanity. So we look away.

But one of the great blessings of loving Austin has been that I can't look away. If we are to make a difference in the world, we have to look at the world and truly see. What we see may be painful, but it is the truth. Not only will it set us free, but it will also strengthen our resolve to do something about it.

Compassion stirs us to remove the pain of the world.
Justice stirs us to remove its cause.

CHAPTER 13

ADJUSTING OUR SAILS

Our new hiring initiative with the enclaves was working in a few isolated ways, but at that point we had no overarching plan, no concrete goals. Eventually a few hundred people with disabilities would have had marginal work at low wages, with no benefits and no future. No one would have blamed us if this was all we accomplished. Quite the opposite—we would have received awards for our good works, and everybody would have considered us fine fellows. Case closed.

By this time, I had put five years into coming up with a way to integrate large numbers of individuals with disabilities into our work environment—first with work-study and now with enclaves. Although the results had been disappointing, I remembered a piece of wisdom from my sailor friends about the unpredictability of weather: "We can't control the wind and the seas, but we can adjust the sails."

We were progressing, and we'd learned a lot along the way, but there were still some adjustments to be made. Work-study was a start but not a permanent solution. Enclaves might have more impact, but they'd never provide the inclusive environment we were hoping for.

It was time to adjust our sails and keep going.

One of our most important lessons about how to adjust came from a man named Chuck in Bethlehem, Pennsylvania. The center's manager had a child with a disability, and the human resources manager had a heart of gold. This was among the first distribution centers to embrace enclaves. So when Chuck, who had Asperger's syndrome, started doing well in the enclave, one of the supervisors thought he might be able to make a go of it on the line. Despite uncertainty about having him integrated as a full-time employee, they offered him the job.

Asperger's syndrome is on the autism spectrum, which meant that Chuck was a lot like Austin—gawky and a bit odd, but not altogether unappealing. He liked repetition, which can be a good thing in a distribution warehouse. And he had incredible focus—another good quality when ten thousand products have to be moved in and out the door every day. Chuck was stationed between two experienced female team members, who became fond of him. He was good at his job—fast and accurate. His social skills weren't the greatest, but the women put out the word that if anybody had a problem with Chuck, that person would have to deal with them. Nobody wanted that.

Things were working out well for everyone. There was one hitch, however. Dancing.

Most of the merchandise is transported in plastic totes, and each distribution center has a unique color so the containers can be returned from the stores to the originating distribution center.

That meant that most of the totes that came down the line were a uniform color. Occasionally, however, a tote from another distribution center would be mixed in. One of our other centers used purple totes, and for reasons known only to him, Chuck delighted in the purple totes. Whenever the occasional purple container came his way, he broke into a dance. He didn't slow down or make mistakes; he just danced. Word spread, and eventually everyone began to look forward to the appearance of a purple tote.

The managers were concerned. *Is dancing allowed?* they asked themselves. Probably not. There

Rules didn't have to rule all the time.

was no rule against it, of course. That's because no one had ever danced on the line before—or ever wanted to, as far as anyone could tell. It was strange, but not dangerous. It wasn't costing the company; it wasn't disrupting work. But it wasn't normal.

Meetings were held. Opinions were aired.

Then the managers decided, "Why not? Let the dancing proceed." After all, it was better to have people dancing than complaining.

When I visited the distribution center, I met Chuck and his two protectors. By then, the center had hired another person with a disability, and he was doing equally well. His father worked at the distribution center too, and he introduced himself to me on my visit. After he told me about his son, he added, "I just wanted to say that if there have to be cutbacks at any time, I'd appreciate it if you would fire me and let my son continue working."

Having found a spot for his son, he didn't want to lose it. He could find another job, but his son might not be able to. I knew how he felt.

Chuck had shown us that someone with a disability could perform the job and meet our standards. In addition, the serendipitous lessons we learned gave me hope that this idea really could work. Although it was a small sample, we saw that people with disabilities could fit in with a group. Coworkers not only accepted Chuck but also engaged him. His presence was a plus to teamwork. Chuck's speed and accuracy were equal to that of the other workers. He was dependable. Plus, his delight in the purple totes gave everyone a lift.

Win-win.

Chuck was the missing piece in the plan. Our successful experience in Bethlehem meant we could start thinking about integrating other individuals with disabilities into the workforce. No more standing on the outside looking in.

But Chuck did more than just show us what people with disabilities could do. He also showed us that typical team members would accept individuals like him more readily than we imagined. He showed us that management could be flexible without giving away the store. Rules didn't have to rule all the time.

While aiming for one victory—integrating people with disabilities into our operation and culture—we uncovered insights we hadn't even seen coming.

Serendipity is the flip side of uncertainty.

CHAPTER 14

PICK YOUR MOMENT

BY THE LATE 1990S, Walgreens was coming off a decade of unprecedented growth. It had taken us ninety years to get to two thousand stores. It took us only ten more to get to three thousand. We were the fastest-growing drugstore chain in the country. And we were just getting started. Over the next decade, we would more than double the number of stores.

When Dan Jorndt, the CEO, described our strategy in dealing with big-box retailers like Walmart and Target, he likened us to a pair of rabbits that were chased down a hole by hounds. One rabbit shivered with fear, but the other rabbit assured him, "Don't worry. If we stay down here long enough, we'll surround 'em!"

Walgreens was building five hundred stores a year, which meant we were going to have to build a number of new distribution centers. As the executive in charge of distribution, I was in the middle of the action. We had seven thousand people working for us in the distribution centers, and that number was about to shoot up. With so much growth taking place, we were truly free to innovate and manage in the ways we thought were best.

Our strategy during the '90s was to build additions to our existing distribution centers under a "bend, don't break" strategy that delayed building new centers as long as possible. By the turn of the century, we were at a breaking point, so we had to build new centers to keep up with the growth. However, the delay had given us time to research and design a new generation of distribution centers that would be bigger and more automated than any facilities we'd ever built.

Typically the most significant cost of building a retail distribution center is the equipment inside that helps move the merchandise, not the external structure. So the cost of automation was a big consideration in determining how much to automate. And automation technology was advancing rapidly. Moore's law, which is often used to describe rapid advances in the semiconductor industry, says that the number of transistors on a chip doubles every two years. Technology generally follows the trend, getting twice as effective and costing half as much. So once again, the longer we delayed committing, the better. The objective of our "bend, don't break" rule was to plan our strategy and hold off long enough to get our distribution centers in the best locations at the lowest cost with the most up-to-date technology, but not to delay so long that existing stores or our growth rate would be hurt.

The new century opened with a dour business outlook. First came the dot-com bust. Then September 11.

We had just opened the first of four new-generation distribution centers in Florida, and a second was well underway in Texas when the country was plunged into uncertainty. Although the spirit of community rose to an unprecedented level in the weeks following the terrorist attacks, the business outlook was dismal as consumers pulled back on their spending. Walgreens looked ahead to "the Christmas that wasn't," and the company's officers met to discuss whether we should defer our plans for growth. Sensing the pessimistic mood, Jorndt looked about the room and said, "Our competitors are sitting around in boardrooms like this and thinking about what they can do to cut back. Here's what we're going to do: we're going to take our money and buy cannonballs to fire into their ships while they're sitting around worrying about how they're going to weather this storm. And when we're done, they won't be able to catch up."

In an instant, the mood and resolve of the room changed. The strategy was simple and clear. And we all knew our parts.

My part was to build the most efficient distribution centers possible. My predecessor, who had served in his role for twenty-five years, had built a distribution system that Walgreens took special pride in believing was the best in the business. Carrying the tradition forward, we visited distribution centers all over the world to make sure we kept our lead. We went to Germany, Japan, and Austria. We brought back the most up-to-date technology and recruited the best companies to help us.

As growth accelerated, pressure mounted for the distribution centers to be more efficient than ever. We finished the center in Texas and built two more. That meant building four huge, state-of-the-art distribution centers in five years—something our company had never done before. The fourth was under way before the first one had even proved out. We streamlined the process so completely that the only difference in the buildings was the paint color and the placement of a column in a conference room. The new technology performed as expected and was so efficient that we were able to get ahead of our store growth in logistics capacity.

That gave us time to catch our breath. We had two more centers to build and the time to plan a newer generation. We could apply what we'd learned from the latest centers, plus take advantage of the technological advances of the last four years.

We started with a blank slate, intending to design the most productive distribution centers of their kind. I can't tell you exactly when a larger vision began to form—there was no specific eureka moment. It was more like I inched my way forward in a state of bedazzlement, enamored with all that our technology could achieve.

Before long this question formed itself completely in my mind: *Why not make them so someone with almost any disability could work for us?* Since the buildings hadn't been designed yet, we could easily make them work for individuals with almost any specific needs. With a new workforce, we wouldn't have to fight entrenched ideas. Since we'd announce our intentions from the beginning, anyone who didn't want to work with individuals with disabilities wouldn't be hired. Each of the two new centers would employ six hundred people. That's a lot of jobs. Surely we could find room for those who might never be offered an opportunity otherwise.

> **Disappointments of the past can be overcome in an instant by a single act of determination.**

It felt like the chance of a lifetime to be able to create the most advanced distribution centers in the world. But even at the time, we knew the greatness of the achievement was fleeting and it wouldn't be long before someone somewhere built something even better. Such is the nature of things—they're all temporal.

But what if we could do something that would demonstrate that people with disabilities could be effective in a commercial setting doing mission-critical work efficiently, safely, and with high quality? We just might have the chance to do something with lasting positive impact.

Greatness and goodness.

I was thinking about all this when I heard a line in a speech that raised our endeavor from the mundane to the poetic. The speaker referred to a time when "hope and history rhyme." I looked up the phrase and found it's by Irish poet laureate Seamus Heaney in his adaptation of an ancient Greek play.

Philoctetes, a Greek warrior, has been injured, disfigured, and abandoned by his comrades on a deserted island in the Aegean Sea. Then one day his former comrades, reaching a point of despair in their war with Troy, remember that Philoctetes has a magic bow. Convinced that his bow is the key to winning the war, they go to the island, find him, and restore him to his former place among the troops. Heaney uses this story to illustrate how the disappointments of the past can be overcome in an instant by a single act of determination. The words seemed to jump off the page as I read them:

> *History says,* Don't hope
> On this side of the grave.
> *But then, once in a lifetime*
> *The longed-for tidal wave*
> *Of justice can rise up,*
> *And hope and history rhyme.*
> *So hope for a great sea-change . . .*
> *Believe that a further shore*
> *Is reachable from here.*
> *Believe in miracles.*
> *And cures and healing wells.*[1]

If there was ever a time for hope and history to rhyme, it was now. And we could be part of it.

As I looked to the future for Walgreens, I also spent some time rewinding to something that had happened in 1985, when I worked for accounting firm Arthur Andersen. I was on a recruiting trip on a college campus where I interviewed an MBA candidate named Robert Bond. Instead of offering the usual tentative handshake, Robert bounded into the booth, slammed his hand on the table, and said, "I want to know what it takes to get hired here, because I've decided that Arthur Andersen is the place for me!" His enthusiasm was contagious, and we hired him.

Robert got off to a good start. Then, just a few months into the job, he decided to go on vacation to Florida. While he was there, he dove off a pier into seventeen inches of water. The dive broke his neck and left him paralyzed except for his head and one arm.

At the time, all our client work was done in the clients' offices. Computers were a rarity then, and it was impossible for Robert to do his job as it had once existed. Arthur Andersen could have easily let him go, especially since he had been with the company less than a year. Instead, they adapted his workstation so he could continue his job. When I asked the partner in charge of administration why they'd gone to so much trouble, he'd replied as if the answer were obvious. "If we can't, who can?"

And now I was asking that same question of myself and Walgreens: *If we can't, who can?* There would never be a better place or a better time. We had the skills, the money, the need, and the drive. It was time to go big.

And maybe it was time for hope and history to rhyme.

It's time to ask yourself, If we can't, who can? Who else will make greatness and goodness rhyme?

CHAPTER 15

BEST PRACTICES

In MANY WAYS, Austin was a pioneer. Our school district had little experience with children who had autism. In one of our early meetings, the school district's new head of special education told us that the district had traditionally transferred students like Austin to specialized facilities in other districts. He wanted to change that but admitted that Austin would be breaking new ground.

Teachers who had observed Austin while he was in early childhood classes believed he could be placed in the special education program for children with disabilities in our local school district. For Austin, this meant he would share music, art, and gym classes with typically abled children—a big step up from the early childhood program he came from. Kay visited the school and spoke to the classes a few days before Austin's arrival. She explained to the children that Austin was born with autism, which meant he had problems communicating. He couldn't say many words, but he understood more. She assured them that autism wasn't contagious—that they couldn't catch it from him. She told them what toys and TV shows Austin liked so they'd know that in many ways he was just like them.

During those years in primary school, Austin surprised us all, and he managed to find his place in the traditional school setting. Although his communication skills were limited, we were grateful to see that his unique personality and humor had a place to emerge.

Like our school district, Walgreens was breaking new ground. If this idea to integrate those with disabilities into our workplace was ever going to take off, I would have to bring others along with me. And so I took a first step: I started talking it up.

One of the people I liked to bounce ideas off was Jeannie Hamilton, the head of human resources for the division. Jeannie had no problem telling me if an idea was dumb, which made her a valuable sounding board—and a good test for my self-esteem.

"Wouldn't it be great if we could employ a large number of people with disabilities and have them function just like other employees—doing the same work and being paid the same wages?" I asked Jeannie.

"Sure," she said non-committally. "It would be great."

"Wouldn't it be great to have them employed at all levels, from loading trucks to management?"

"That would be great," she said.

"What would we need to do to make that happen?"

"Well," she said, "we'd need to figure out what employees in the distribution centers need to be capable of in order to do their jobs."

"Right," I said. We started a list.

Would they need to be able to read?

Would they have to follow instructions?

Would they have to be able to work as a team?

I noodled with the idea over the next couple of weeks, sketching out what it would take for these employees to be successful. Two weeks later, I dropped by her office again.

"Have you been thinking about that idea?" I asked.

She had.

Thus began the second of many conversations that would lead us to define, redefine, examine, interpret, and sometimes reinvent the tasks and policies required to run a distribution center. This idea would grow far beyond us, and later, dozens, then hundreds, and eventually thousands of people would get involved. And it would finally be led by the unlikeliest of champions—big business.

> **"Time is the greatest innovator."**
>
> —FRANCIS BACON

But for now, we had to get people on board—one individual at a time.

The next person we pulled into the project was our training expert, Karen Preston. She began looking for companies that were already doing what we planned to do. We didn't care as much about the specifics of what these companies were doing as the fact that they were making this work. We wanted confirmation that we weren't completely crazy.

Karen found a few small-company entrepreneurs who employed a relatively large percentage of individuals with disabilities in their workforce. One of them was Carolina Fine Snacks in Greensboro, North Carolina. Half of the company's twenty factory workers had visual impairments or hearing loss or cognitive disabilities.

Before these workers came on board, one in five employees failed to come to work on a given day, and their productivity averaged only 50 to 60 percent of expectations. Then the owner, Phil Kosak, attended an employment fair for people with disabilities and decided to hire some of these individuals. Over the course of six months, employee turnover dropped from 80 percent to less than 5 percent, and productivity rose by more than 50 percent. Absenteeism dropped from 20 percent to less than 5 percent. Worker tardiness dropped from 30 percent to zero.

Habitat International in Chattanooga was another success story. Seventy-five percent of employees in this small manufacturer of indoor/outdoor carpeting had disabilities. The program, launched by owner David Morris, also included recovering alcoholics, homeless people, and non-English speakers. Morris openly advocated a business philosophy of love, kindness, and compassion. Habitat's workers regularly outproduced the competition two to one.

Karen found a number of large companies that hired one or two individuals with disabilities, but nobody aggressively recruited in the way we wanted to. A widespread initiative to pay equal wages for those with disabilities and expect equal work was unheard of at most corporations. Since big companies weren't in the game, we didn't have models to follow, but I wasn't going to let that stop us. I reasoned that starting from the ground up would give us a chance to develop our own model.

Businesses often search for "best practices" to learn from and emulate. The Walgreens attitude had always been to be aware of trends and technology but not worry much about benchmarking ourselves against the competition. We wanted to be the innovators our competitors were chasing. Our path followed the example of legendary basketball coach John Wooden, whose teams won an unprecedented seven NCAA championships in a row. He never bothered to scout out the competition, instead concentrating on making his team the best it could be.

We were about to consider something that never had been done before. That gave us pause, but it didn't deter us. We only had to look back on the history of innovation to see that our idea might be possible. New discoveries often come from applying known concepts and methods in different ways to reveal that something once thought impossible is now a reality. As Francis Bacon observed, "Time is the greatest innovator." Perhaps our initiative was an idea whose time had come.

When people say "best practice," think best practice so far. If no one has ever done something before, that's an opportunity, not a stop sign.

CHAPTER 16

LEADERS GO BEFORE THEIR TROOPS

THE WORK IN a distribution center is fast: everything is focused on getting the work done well, on schedule, and at the lowest possible cost. Minutes and pennies count. The work is also physical and potentially dangerous, as employees are lifting boxes, wielding box cutters, and dodging machinery. Speed, efficiency, safety—that's DC culture.

So when we started contemplating hiring people with disabilities, it seemed counter-intuitive to those inherent distribution values. We would not only have to get on board ourselves; we'd also have to convince other parts of the company, including the CEO and board members.

In our research, we'd found only small companies with impressive track records of hiring people with disabilities, because change, innovation, and creativity are easier to effect in small companies. Small, privately owned companies tend to be more nimble—they can change quickly and then adapt just as quickly when a change isn't working. Unencumbered by layers of managers and staff between the corner office and the shop floor, management can decree a new course of action and follow up to make sure it happens.

Small companies are speedboats; a company as massive as Walgreens is an ocean liner. Turning the ship requires time, planning, and decisions coordinated across many departments. I could decree changes within the distribution centers, but my edicts might be sabotaged at a hundred levels just within my own area. Outside my functional area, the problem was infinitely greater. I had only moral suasion, and I needed the cooperation of many departments: human resources, legal, engineering—the list went on. Each department had goals of its own, a full workload, and only so much time. Add to that limited resources, limited energy, and turf wars that can derail any new plan, and it quickly becomes obvious how difficult any change, much less one as radical as this one, can be.

I knew I couldn't do this alone—I would need those around me to get on board.

In large companies, it's common practice to say no to anything new—and in some places, no is an automatic. I was given countless reasons why hiring large numbers of individuals with disabilities wouldn't work, and for every reason I heard, ten more were being discussed outside my hearing. I knew all these concerns would hinder our initiative. But Jeannie, Karen, and I had a vision that was growing stronger every day.

When my optimism flagged, I told myself, *Remember Joan of Arc.*

Joan, an uneducated French peasant girl, had a vision that she would lead France's revolt against English domination. France had been at war with England for years—a war so drawn out it became known as the Hundred Years' War. France hadn't fared well in the initial phases, failing to win a single battle. The French had even lost Orléans—the city where Charles was to be crowned king.

Joan was quite vocal about her sense of destiny, and word spread. Eventually the local garrison commander granted her an escort to help her navigate enemy-held land, and she rode off to see the king. She told the king of her vision, and having nothing to lose, he sent her to join his generals.

The story is told that in her first meeting with the war council that was strategizing how to take back the city of Orléans, Joan said they should attack the city straight on. The seasoned generals said her approach had been attempted before and had failed. They believed the best approach would be to lay the city under siege and starve out the English. But Joan was adamant. "Attack!" she said. She knew it was the only way to win.

The generals countered that if she attacked, she would attack alone. No one would follow her.

"Then I won't look back," she replied.

The next day, with the entire army watching, she was first on the field, as promised. And she carried with her not a sword but the banner of France. The generals were wrong that no one would follow her. The French army rose up behind her, and she led them to a grand victory.

Early on Kay and I realized that if others were to accept our son without fearing him, we would have to be his Joan of Arc—out front and fearless. We could never play the role of "poor, pitiful parent." If we wanted people to think him capable, we had to demonstrate our confidence in him first.

Knowing Austin's uncanny sense of direction, we never expressed concern when he wandered off at church, and we never followed him once he learned to ride a bike. When he reached the minimum height requirement at the local amusement park, we let him drive go-karts with the rest of the family. If others questioned his odd mannerisms, we explained them in a matter-of-fact manner, as if discussing an eccentric but beloved uncle. Our reward was that our church, our neighbors, and his teachers embraced him as one of their own.

When it came down to it, my role wasn't that different with regard to the Walgreens initiative. I knew that even my most loyal supporters had some doubts. And I wasn't blind to the possibility of failure. But I also knew I couldn't do this alone—I would need those around me to get on board. If they were going to join me, they first needed to know I was willing to take risks myself and bear the burden of failure. That comes with the territory when you're the one out front.

True leaders know where they're going. Go in front of the troops—showing the way, not pushing them from behind.

CHAPTER 17

I'D BETTER SEE SOME DINOSAURS

ONE OF OUR most heated discussions as we tried to get our initiative off the ground cropped up over how to define a disability. Jeannie pointed out that we'd been focusing on physical and cognitive disabilities but that, according to the law, drug and alcohol addictions were also considered disabilities. Depression counted, and so did attention deficit disorder. Anger management was a disability; so was diabetes.

As Jeannie went through the list, I began to shake my head. Jeannie thought I was objecting to the idea of including so many diagnoses in the category of disability. Not exactly. I was thinking that we probably already had a number of team members with those disabilities; it was just easier to hide them than something like autism or cerebral palsy. I could point to my own mother, who had worked successfully since I was five despite a lifetime of diagnosed depression that resulted in electric shock treatments and occasional barbiturate and alcohol abuse.

If we were aiming for only those who could pass as "normal," we weren't doing anything different from what we'd been doing before. We needed big goals that would demand our best efforts. In frustration, I reminded everyone of the scene in *Jurassic Park* in which the visiting scientist played by Jeff Goldblum is invited on a preopening tour of the park. As the automated vehicle full of visitors passes through various areas, there are no dinosaurs to be seen. Goldblum says something like, "Are there dinosaurs on this dinosaur tour?"

> **We needed big goals that would demand our best efforts.**

We weren't going to exclude any disability at the expense of another. And we would accommodate as many people as we could. We ended in agreement with one final caution: "When we walk through the distribution center, there'd better be some dinosaurs."

Know what you're aiming for. Don't get sidetracked into a lesser dream.

CHAPTER 18

MANAGE YOUR FEAR

FOLLOWING OUR POLICY of aiming high, our initial focus was to hire people with autism. Having witnessed Austin's experiences and struggles, I thought these individuals would be among the most difficult to employ—and the hardest to train. Our son had been practically uncontrollable until we'd discovered the magic of time-outs. And even then, we needed to employ those interventions without deviation day after day after day.

How long had it taken us to teach Austin to tie his shoes? Forever. How long had it taken before he used a toilet? Forever. How long had it taken for him to learn to drive? Forever. Okay—two years that *seemed* like forever.

We figured that if we could succeed with people like Austin, we could succeed with anyone. Plus, the reality of autism was coming at society like a tsunami, affecting one out of about every hundred children born.[1] Not since the fear of polio had a condition affected so many families. Except that this time there was no cure in sight.

One of our concerns was that people with autism would require a number of additional staff to support them. We hoped, however, that our environment would be so inclusive that coworkers would help train and support each other without disrupting their own performance. I later learned that this philosophy is called "natural support" in the disability employment community. I asked disability expert James Emmett how many typically abled team members we would need to support a fellow team member with autism. He thought for a moment and said, "Two, probably."

We now had our hiring goal. One out of three team members would be individuals with disabilities. In a workforce of six hundred employees whose activities had to be synchronized throughout the day across the entire distribution center, two hundred of these would be individuals with disabilities. It was an astounding number—and an exciting challenge. As the legendary nineteenth-century architect Daniel Burnham once said, "Make no little plans; they have no magic to stir men's blood."

As Karen began sharing our plans with disability experts, she was told that people with autism wouldn't be fast enough or accurate enough. They wouldn't be able to work full shifts. They would tire and lose concentration. And social skills? Forget about it, the experts said.

Some people would have to be taught to come to work on time. Then they would have to be taught to leave on time. They would have to be instructed about how to take breaks and then shown what to do on their breaks. Many would have to be coached on how to make eye contact, shake hands, and say hello. They would need to learn to speak up and then learn to stop talking. Typically abled people watch, copy, and adapt. But the process isn't so straightforward for those with autism.

In addition, abstract concepts can prove frustrating for individuals with autism. If you want to teach them to count money, don't use play money. When they see the real stuff, the lessons with play money won't mean a thing.

At one of Austin's speech sessions, his therapist was working with him on developing his abstract thinking abilities. Phyllis read him a story about astronauts who were preparing for travel to Mars. She asked Austin, "Why do you think people would want to go to Mars?"

Austin hesitated, obviously struggling to come up with an answer.

She prompted, "If you don't know for sure, start with 'Maybe.' You could say, 'Maybe they are going because . . .'" She paused, hoping he'd pick up the cue.

"Maybe?" Austin said. "I hate maybe!"

We knew we'd have to be precise with every single directive. When we said we wanted something clean, what exactly did *clean* mean? A person with autism might spend all day making sure every speck of dirt had been removed from a floor.

Distribution center managers and supervisors tend to be what we call "drivers." They're task oriented—they move product, and they move it quickly, safely, and on time. They don't spend a lot of time thinking about people and their problems. If they liked thinking about people and their problems, they'd have gone into human resources. If they liked cajoling and persuading, they'd have gone into sales. But no, they like getting things done. They sometimes bark out orders. They might yell on occasion. They worry about "making rate" far more than they worry about hurting anyone's feelings.

But a manager who yelled at a team member with autism

> "Make no little plans; they have no magic to stir men's blood."
>
> —DANIEL BURNHAM

might not get compliance—or even a response. The employee might simply walk away. Or if he were like my son, he might be so crushed by the manager's anger that he would continue to feel grieved and afraid for weeks after the incident.

As we became more aware of all the obstacles we were facing, my own fears multiplied. But I kept them to myself, especially at work. Others' trust in the vision would be critical to its success. If I didn't believe in it, no one would. Any expression of fear would encourage doubt, which could cause our team to ease off instead of pushing ahead when the difficulties seemed insurmountable. Pessimism is a self-fulfilling prophecy.

You need to manage your own fear before you can help others manage theirs.

CHAPTER 19

CASH IN YOUR CHIPS

I HAD BEEN before the Walgreens board of directors many times to seek approval for building distribution centers and other large-scale projects. But I'd never presented a proposal with the reach and daring of the plan we brought before them in the summer of 2003. We wanted to spend $180 million doing something nobody had ever considered doing before.

I'd talked through our plans with both Dan Jorndt and David Bernauer, who had replaced Jorndt as CEO. They were both on board. We had done the analysis from all angles to ensure that the project made good business sense. However, at this point we were taking it on faith that sufficient numbers of individuals with disabilities could be recruited and trained to work productively. I was so confident in the rightness of the cause and in our ability to make this happen that I decided to let the eloquence of the plan speak for itself. Instead of the slides and complex analyses that usually accompany major projects, I presented only a one-page financial summary. My presentation was more basic than it was brilliant or inspiring.

"This will be the most automated and cost-effective distribution center in our history," I said.

I looked at the directors around the room. They were all nodding.

"It will be the most expensive DC we have ever built, and it will have the most advanced technology," I went on. "But it will also have a higher return on investment than less-expensive and less-automated alternatives."

They nodded again, though not as quickly this time.

"A large percentage of the workforce will have a disability and likely won't have had the chance to work before," I said. "But they will be held to the same standards as other employees and will be paid the same. They will perform the same jobs and work side by side with those who don't have disabilities."

We had done the analysis to ensure that the project made good business sense. However, there were some things we had to take on faith.

Nobody nodded. I waited a few seconds, which seemed like an eternity.

Finally one director asked, "What if it doesn't work?"

"There is time between now and then to know if it will work or not," I answered. "And if it doesn't work, we'll adjust our goals."

A few more seconds passed as I waited for follow-up questions. Silence. At last one of the directors said, "Thank you."

Dave Bernauer asked if there were other questions. There weren't. Then someone moved the motion and they voted their approval. They thanked me, and I was dismissed.

I'll never know for sure, but I suspect Dave had greased the skids. It was the first of many times when things just seemed to fall into place.

Years later I spoke with Dave about the meeting and thanked him again for taking a chance on it.

He said simply, "I didn't think it was much of a risk, given all your division had achieved in the years leading up to it."

It was time to cash in our chips.

Competence is like money that keeps earning interest.
One day you can cash it in for an even bigger prize.

CHAPTER 20

CATHEDRAL BUILDERS

Now IT WAS time for the work to begin in earnest. We set a completion date for the new distribution center for two years in the future. German engineers headed by a stubborn Dutchman descended on our Deerfield, Illinois, headquarters to hammer out the design. Over the next few months, data was collected, spreadsheet models were created, and voices were occasionally raised as the vision for the building started to go from idea to plan. Teams dealing with software, engineering, and construction had to be coordinated across three continents. People in Germany would design a crane, it would be built in Austria, our people in Deerfield would spell out how it should operate, translators in India would convert our instructions into software, and people in Romania would use the software to control the crane as it moved up and down the aisles to extract a specific box.

Some of the equipment that would be used in our centers had never been made before. On a visit to the factory in Austria, where a lot of the equipment would be custom manufactured, I asked to meet with the workers on the factory floor who would be making it. Although our hosts thought it was an odd request, the employees were gathered and politely assembled in a corner of the factory. Having been pulled away from their work to hear from a foreigner who didn't speak a word of German, they looked understandably uncomfortable.

With the help of a translator, I told them that the machines they were creating would give opportunities to those who had never been given a chance to have a paying job and that their creations would allow these workers to perform as well as anyone in the world. It would serve as a model for other businesses to learn from. This vision couldn't be achieved without them, and I expressed my gratitude on behalf of all the families who couldn't be there to thank them personally.

During the translations, I watched the workers' faces shift from reserve to full attention. People who had listened with crossed arms visibly relaxed. Some leaned forward to listen more intently. Without understanding a word of German, I felt a change come over the room. We were no longer strangers doing a job; we were men and women coming together to do something important—something to make a difference in other people's lives. It was the kind of moment you never forget. These employees were no longer technicians, mechanics, and millwrights assigned to a project. They were on a mission to change the world.

> **We were no longer strangers doing a job; we were men and women coming together to do something important.**

Use every opportunity to help others see meaning in their work. They will be transformed from bricklayers to cathedral builders.

CHAPTER 21

CROSSING THE RUBICON

SOME OF THE machines we selected for our high-tech center had been deployed as stand-alone units but had never been put together to work on a large scale. Our partner in Austria rented an empty warehouse that stood on the grounds of an abandoned chicken processing plant near Graz, and there we were able to build a test set of four workstations—three stories high and a hundred feet long. No one had ever tested more than two workstations together before. The new distribution center would have twenty-four stations. When the line was ready, we assembled our team of engineers, software specialists, and operations leaders and headed off to Austria to test the equipment.

We arrived in the dead of winter and made our way to the unheated building. Bundled against the cold, we shuttled from place to place under a dull winter sky. In a Tim Burton–like setting of machinery whirling and spinning, we pushed boxes around, measured how far the human arm could reach, and tested noise levels. To simulate the weight of products that would be transported by the machines, we loaded plastic totes with sand. The machines ran continuously for days. We worked in coats and hats and gloves, having a glorious time despite the freezing conditions. We'd work until we were too cold to stand it and then run to an adjoining room with a space heater and a chalkboard, where we warmed up and shared new ideas that had come to us.

Whenever we discussed people with disabilities, cost was the elephant in the room. We all agreed that spending extra money to accommodate those with disabilities was impermissible. No one had to say so—it just was.

My "crossing the Rubicon" moment came one day when I was meeting with our engineers to go over a workstation layout. I suggested that to make it easier for someone with a physical disability, we should reduce the distance a person had to reach to do the job.

Ed Grant, our lead engineer, looked across the table and asked, "Are we intentionally building this facility for the disabled?"

We'd never said it like that before. No one had asked such a blunt question out loud. I could have ducked the question by saying that the change would make it easier for everybody, disability or not. My mind raced for what seemed like an eternity.

He waited.

Finally I looked at him straight on. "Yes."

"Okay," he replied simply.

And we moved on.

I felt like Chuck Yeager, the first person to break the sound barrier. Many pilots before him had crashed in the turbulence that comes when approaching supersonic speed. He will always be remembered for making it through the seemingly impenetrable wall of opposing force that forms as sound waves gather in front of an aircraft.

The barrier I'd crossed felt much the same. And like Yeager, I felt a euphoric peace once the barrier was crossed. All the noise and buffeting were left behind. Fears and doubts were gone. Now I could concentrate fully on the job at hand. Success or failure, I was at peace with myself.

From that day forward, our team considered the impact on a person with a disability in every decision we made. If we could reasonably accommodate a disability, we would.

It was much easier to share the idea of hiring people with disabilities than to openly state my commitment to doing it. However, by committing, I had staked out the territory. I'd crossed a clearly defined line, and now others would choose whether or not to join me.

Fears and doubts were now gone. Success or failure, I was at peace with myself.

At the very least, I would know who would be standing with me.

A public commitment lets everyone know which side of the line they stand on. The leader must be the first to cross the line.

CHAPTER 22

ELIMINATE FEAR

EVERYBODY SAYS YOU can't change the world. But that's exactly what all of us want to do. So that became the focus—changing the world. At first I just said it to myself; then I started saying it to other people. Once again, some scoffed, but others caught the fire.

In our attempt to employ people with disabilities, we couldn't pretend success was guaranteed. But if we were going to have a shot at achieving our goal, we needed to aim high. I'd learned from my other attempts to employ people with disabilities that setting the bar low wasn't going to get us anywhere. People want to be inspired, to be reminded that they are capable of great things—even changing the world.

If we were going to be successful, we would have to address the obstacle that stands in the way of every great undertaking: fear. A certain amount of fear is endemic to business because uncertainty comes with the territory in any industry. It's not a question of whether fear is there; it's only a question of how much—and how we respond to it. Leaders must work consciously, constantly, and conspicuously to drive out fear.

I know fear firsthand. Fear of failure. Fear of looking bad or appearing weak. Fear of losing respect or position. Fear has kept me quiet in the past when I should have spoken up. It has kept me still when I should have acted.

Most execs underestimate how much fear is present in their organizations. Some view fear as a way to impose their will on others; a few even think it's a way to get respect. But that depends on how you define respect. I respect those I fear in the same way I respect rattlesnakes—the only difference is that I don't abhor rattlesnakes.

Fear undermines trust, commitment, and creativity, and unfortunately I have seen this unfold in my own life. I once saw a long-time employee with a proven track record of success present a plan to a newly hired vice president. At the conclusion of the meeting, the vice president had no comments or questions except this one: "Are you willing to bet your job on your plan?"

> **Leaders must work consciously, constantly, and conspicuously to drive out fear.**

This fear-based approach stands in contrast to my first presentation to Dan Jorndt when he became president. The project I was responsible for was way behind schedule, and I reported the bad news along with a plan for going forward. Jorndt listened intently throughout my presentation, and then, as the meeting concluded and everyone got up to leave, Jorndt walked over to me. He put his arm around my shoulders like a coach would do for a quarterback who was about to go into the game with the winning play. He said, "I hope you have big shoulders, Randy. Because we sure are going to need them."

Jorndt's dad must have taught him the same lesson my dad had taught me—that people will do more if they're worried about disappointing you than if they're afraid of you. After that meeting, I made sure I did everything possible to be worthy of Jorndt's faith in me. I gave him my best.

If we were going to achieve something of this scale without precedent, we needed to get the best out of everyone on the team. And the way to make sure we were getting everyone's best was to make sure we were motivating people with a vision, not with fear.

While fear only stands in the way, a clear vision inspires. While fear makes us try to avoid a loss, vision encourages us to take healthy risks. While fear makes us want to hedge our bets, vision emboldens. While fear leads us to run out the clock, vision helps us draw up a good play and score a touchdown.

If we were going to change the world, we had to be playing to win. Nothing less would get us there.

Drive out fear. It stands in the way of greatness.

CHAPTER 23

SHARE THE STORY

As I MOUNTED the main stage in the grand ballroom of the Paris Las Vegas Hotel to tell our story to more than five thousand Walgreens store managers, I was very aware that a distribution guy had never spoken at the national store manager meeting before.

Stores are the heart of the company. No surprise, since that's where 90 percent of the employees work and where the profits come from. If the company were a body, stores would be its face, hands, and voice. Other parts of the company may believe they are the brain, but they know better than to claim it within earshot of store people.

The store operations culture is fiercely loyal. Working in retail stores is a little like playing hockey: every day is different, and you can never rest on your laurels. All our CEOs for the past hundred years had begun their careers in Walgreens stores and worked their way up. The only way to the corner office is through the stores.

The confab in Las Vegas was reserved for down-to-earth topics for store managers to make their stores more profitable. This audience wanted to know which key items they would be adding to their inventory and how next year's merchandising plans were going to work. These were not touchy-feely gatherings with fluff topics and a lot of free time. The meetings cost millions of dollars just for the airfare, food, and rooms (two store managers per room, of course). We didn't want to waste a penny on frivolous expenses.

Until that day, most of my encounters with stores had been transactional. The most frequent questions store managers asked of my department went something like this: "Where is this item we ordered?" "Why are we out of stock on this?" "Why is my truck always late?" It was with some trepidation that I approached the stage in the center of the huge auditorium, surrounded by people who may have heard my name only when it was attached to a problem. Although I was a senior vice president and one of the company's highest-ranking officers, in that meeting I was more a wary guest than a dignitary.

My intention for the speech was that it would be a sort of payback. In talks with team members at the distribution centers, I'd often given their work its proper context by sharing stories of heroic efforts made by our stores in serving customers. Now we were coming full circle: I was going to tell team members from the stores what their work was enabling the centers to do.

I'd practiced what I was going to say a hundred times, but I was still nervous as I headed up the stairs to the stage. I started out by briefly telling the audience that we were going to have an entirely new generation of distribution centers—buildings designed to lower costs, respond more quickly, and be more flexible in getting them merchandise so they could have lower prices and better profits. With the new centers, it would be easier to keep items in stock, which meant we would avoid those stockouts the stores hated.

They sat politely. I talked about how cool the automation

would be and showed them a short video of the equipment. They'd have been just as interested if I had shown a video of a farmer churning butter.

Then I made the big announcement: "One-third of the workforce in our new distribution centers will be people with disabilities." It was the first time I'd made this announcement and mentioned a specific percentage of hires. I'm sure many people gulped when they heard that, but it got their attention.

Then a picture of my family came on the screen. I told them about Austin, about the challenges he faced, about the fears of a parent whose child has a disability, about our hope to live one day longer than our child.

"Despite the efforts of parents, teachers, and therapists," I continued, "nearly 70 percent of individuals with disabilities and 95 percent of people with severe cognitive disabilities such as Austin's will never hold down a job.

"When it comes to employment, people with special needs die from a thousand cuts: they look different, they don't interview well, they probably aren't able to drive to work, and they don't learn in the ways employers are used to teaching," I said. "But the unkindest cut of all is that no matter what they can do and how well they can do it, we employers rarely give them a chance."

The initiative to hire people with disabilities had gone from being my cause to being our cause.

I looked around the room, trying to gauge the reaction of the crowd. "Businesses believe that hiring a person with a disability is a nice thing to do if you can afford it. It's charity—good business from a public relations standpoint, but not something that's going to help the bottom line. But Walgreens is going to change all that."

I showed them a picture of our eleven-person enclave in our Madison, Wisconsin, distribution center. Two people were in wheelchairs; one person wore a protective helmet; two had canes. None had those easy, practiced smiles you see in high school yearbooks, but they were all smiling.

"These people and thousands of others like them are waiting on the margins of society. Waiting for an opportunity. Waiting to belong," I went on. "We're going to do this with the kind of commitment and savvy that no one else has attempted before."

I shared about the more than one hundred Walgreens team members who had already been working full time for more than a year to make this initiative successful.

Then I looked into the faces of the store managers and said pointedly, "If this is going to work, we're going to need the help of departments across the company."

I wanted them to realize that although most of us in that room didn't have a visible disability, those who did weren't as different as they might seem to be. My family's story wasn't an isolated experience. It was different only in the specifics.

As my speech drew to a close, I took a chance. "Will all those in the audience who have a son or daughter, a relative, or a neighbor with a disability—anyone who holds someone with a disability in his or her heart—please stand up?"

Slowly people began to rise. All at once, the usual rustling that comes in a group of five thousand people stopped, and the auditorium was blanketed in silence. The quiet began to take on an almost sacred reverence as more and more people stood. It wasn't long before about a thousand people were standing.

It was an astounding moment. These people hadn't just heard the words I'd spoken; they'd seen the words.

The initiative to hire people with disabilities had gone from being my cause to being our cause. It wasn't just a story about "those people" with disabilities; they saw themselves in the story.

Help people see themselves in the story, and it will become their story too.

CHAPTER 24

WHERE THE BUCK STOPS

Until the meeting in Vegas, our project had been known to only a limited number of people. Up to that point, we could have backed off our ambitious targets without fanfare, claiming that circumstances had changed. After the meeting, however, thousands of people knew about the plan—and they were excited about it. This was no longer something that would be allowed to die a quiet death. If it failed, it would fail in a big, public way.

Now that it was real, we had a lot to do in a relatively short time. The first site had to be selected and secured. The building needed to be erected, equipment needed to be installed, and software had to be tested.

The management team for the new distribution center wasn't in place yet either—we still needed to recruit managers and then train them for their unique responsibilities. Most important, we had to find, train, and hire a workforce—the majority of whom had no prior experience in a distribution center. For many of our new hires with special needs, it would be their first job of any kind.

Success would require the coordinated work of many departments across the company—real estate, human resources, legal, construction, training, engineering, purchasing, operations. Not an easy task.

Interdepartmental cooperation is always difficult in large, bureaucratic organizations. As I've already mentioned, "Just say no" could be the slogan for everything in the corporate world. Stalling, evading, and outright refusals to comply are common—and the more people you have involved, the more trouble you have getting anything done. Turf wars can break out over any number of issues. Too much work. Too little work. Lines of authority. Lack of authority. At Walgreens we had this saying: "We issue more brake handles than accelerators."

If we were going to pull off our project, people in departments across the company would need to shake off old ways and innovate.

> **Bolstered by the knowledge that my boss had confidence I would do the right thing, I found my increased responsibility more liberating than fearsome.**

Fortunately, I had not only the responsibility for the outcome but also the authority to direct the resources needed to achieve the expected results. Knowing I would be responsible for the outcome, other people were freed from the fear of taking risks. If I approved an expenditure or a policy that failed, I would take the hit. Bolstered by the knowledge that my boss had confidence I would do the right thing, I found my increased responsibility more liberating than fearsome. I was determined to move heaven and earth, if necessary, so I wouldn't disappoint him.

About this time, disability expert Deb Russell joined the company. It turned out to be a fortunate turn of events for us, as Karen retired and Jeannie got married and moved away a few months later. Deb came on board because she knew we were serious about hiring people with disabilities. But although she thought our goals were admirable, she privately thought we would fall way short of achieving them. Her experience had taught her that hiring people with disabilities was something companies talked about more than they actually did. Even in ideal circumstances, some difficulty tends to arise that undermines the best of intentions—a change of managers, a shift in priorities, budget constraints.

Direct and quick-witted, Deb would occasionally test the extent of my commitment. Early on in the process, she wanted to know if we were going to limit the types of disabilities that we would accommodate. Invoking the politically incorrect pejorative to rattle me, she asked, "Are we going to hire crazies?"

"We'll cross that bridge when we come to it," I answered. I didn't want to close any doors on anyone at that point. Plus, arbitrary exclusions would diminish the vision and open the door for the team to second-guess my commitment. They already had enough doubts of their own.

Perhaps it was because people weren't afraid of being blamed for failure, or perhaps it was because they believed in the goals we hoped to achieve, but whatever the case, an odd thing happened during this process of getting the distribution centers ready. Seemingly insurmountable barriers would dissolve before they became problems. Managers, who are often considered difficult to deal with in such situations, became helpful. Departmental lines evaporated. People worked together creatively. I was amazed at how the disparate pieces started to come together.

Giving others the authority to get the job done sped up decision making and engaged people more fully. There is a subtle difference between authority and responsibility, in that authority can be delegated to others. Responsibility, on the other hand, is assignable but not transferable. For instance, if my boss assigns me the responsibility to get something done, I am ultimately accountable to him or her for the result. I can hold others accountable to me, but I cannot pass my own accountability to them.

Retaining responsibility has its advantages. In our case, it kept the goals from being co-opted when conflicts or difficulties arose along the way. More important, it provided clarity and political cover for the rest of the team.

We can delegate authority but not responsibility.

CHAPTER 25

THE JOURNEY IS WORTH IT

EVEN THOUGH OUR expectations had been set high, we couldn't lose sight of the ground rules. We had to be fair to all our stakeholders—shareholders, management, team members, customers. We knew that many would be skeptical about hiring people with disabilities. After all, we were a business, not a charity. We were businesspeople, not social workers. It was our job to keep the trucks rolling. No delays. No mistakes.

The technology was not virgin territory for us. We knew how to get machines to do amazing things. We knew how to modify software. People, on the other hand, were another kind of problem altogether.

Building the workforce and figuring out how we were going to manage it would be far more difficult than implementing technology. Ever since we'd gone public with our plan that one-third of the distribution staff would be individuals with disabilities, things had become very real. Fear and its ugly brother, doubt, began to rear their heads. Potential problems came out of the woodwork. We addressed them—sometimes with comical results.

In one meeting this question came up: "How will a deaf person know that a janitor is about to enter the restroom? Or how will a deaf janitor know that the restroom is occupied?"

"Maybe we could have the janitor roll a tennis ball into the restroom and the person inside could roll it back," someone suggested.

This raised some eyebrows. "But what if the person couldn't reach it to roll it back?"

After a pause another person offered, "We could equip each stall with something like a small hockey stick!" They say there are no dumb ideas in a brainstorming session, but this one came pretty close.

Finally someone said, "Why don't we use men to clean the men's rooms and women to clean the women's rooms and see how it works?" Simple. Elegant.

As it turned out, however, even when we thought we weren't overthinking it, we were. Years later, when I followed up to see how the process was working, a team member told me that if needed, the janitor asks a team member of the same gender to check the restroom first. Sometimes worry about the future makes things more complicated than they need to be.

Our own experience at home with Austin had taught me that many of the scenarios we imagine with dread never happen. When we thought about Austin's future, we envisioned a grown man who had to be wrestled down for haircuts and kept locked in the house so he wouldn't run off. That man never appeared. Austin finally started speaking. He could tie his shoes. He didn't run off and get in accidents or get kidnapped by monsters.

There were problems that we didn't anticipate, of course. Getting him to take his medicine on time. Tending to his hygiene. Dealing with puberty. Monitoring his diet. Teaching him daily living skills. All the real problems were more mundane and less dramatic than the ones we'd imagined.

Uncertainty makes people jittery. The best question someone brought up at one of our planning meetings was "What about the problems we haven't thought of?" I assured everyone that unforeseen problems weren't just a possibility but a certainty and that we would address those occasions as they came up.

So many imaginary problems started surfacing that I made two rules. The first was "Don't bring up a problem until you have at least one solution or a way to work around it." And based on my own experience that the fear of failure is

> **Many of the scenarios we imagine with dread never happen.**

often the underlying reason for all the what-ifs, the second rule was "Don't worry about failing." Success or failure, this would be the best work of our lives and the thing we'd be most proud of. When it came to our disability-hiring initiative, we would achieve a lot even if we fell short of our target. I often found myself quoting the familiar saying: "Anything worth doing is worth doing poorly."

We were doing something new, with few precedents to guide us. This meant that we would have to deal with uncertainty and depend on discovery along the way. It was more like blazing a new trail than like making the morning commute.

Innovation is a journey, not a commute.

CHAPTER 26

BUCKING THE STATUS QUO

Even though we would have problems we couldn't anticipate, I had a secret weapon. Life with Austin.

The experts had been quite specific about what Austin would likely never be able to do. But when it came time to tell us what he *would* be able to do, they were either maddeningly vague or discouragingly pessimistic. He might never be potty trained. He might never tie his own shoes. Would he learn to read? We'd have to see. Would he learn to swim? Who knew? In fact, he learned to do all those things.

About the time we were beginning to search for sites for the new distribution center, Austin turned sixteen. We had been told that he would never drive. But knowing what it would mean for Austin's future independence and remembering that he had once raced around the go-kart track just like the other kids, we wouldn't give up on the idea that he might drive after all.

When we asked that Austin be allowed to take the driver's education test, the head of the special education program at his school expressed doubt that he could drive safely and advised us against pursuing it. We persisted. She insisted on an independent evaluation of his cognitive skills before letting him enroll. It was the first of many hurdles in the process, and I admit to holding my breath as we waited for the results. But when he completed the evaluation successfully, I wasn't entirely surprised.

Austin also passed the driver's education class with flying colors. Just to be sure, we had him take the class again. Again he passed, which meant he earned a learner's permit. Austin became our "undercover" student driver as he and I drove through the neighborhood late at night. We also hired a private instructor named Mr. Valencia. We told him that Austin was concerned about doing a good job and that praise would mitigate some of our son's stress. After the first lesson, we asked if Austin had done well. Mr. Valencia affirmed that he had, and as we'd promised, our son responded well to the praise. He said Austin also gave him praise for being a good instructor—something none of his other students had ever done. Mr. Valencia noted that the positive feedback made him feel good too.

> **Even people with great knowledge and the best of intentions can hold us back if we let them.**

A few weeks later, Kay took Austin for his driving test. As I waited at work to hear the results, it was hard to concentrate on anything else. I was thinking that for Austin, getting a driver's license would be like graduating summa cum laude from MIT. Getting a job that would allow him to live independently would be like winning a Nobel Prize. First the license, then the job. Maybe. Someday. When Kay called and said that he'd passed without a hitch, I bent my head in gratitude. What most kids do in less than a year, Austin had taken two years to do. So what? Two years were a whole lot better than never.

But the story gets even better. Austin went on to become my chauffeur, and he now drives me through Chicago traffic to the airport. For twenty dollars, Austin is ready to give me a ride whenever I need to catch a flight. He's never late. He never complains about the inconvenience. He does complain about the traffic, but so do I. I take it as a good sign that in some ways he's just like the rest of us.

When we get to the airport, I always say, "Austin, you did a really good job. Thank you so much. I love you, and I'll see you when I get back."

Austin always responds in a matter-of-fact voice, "Twenty dollars." Social graces are still not Austin's forte.

The only thing unusual about Austin's driving is that, given the chance, he will avoid the traffic lights that are equipped with automated cameras—the ones used to ticket drivers who run red lights. Once we got a traffic ticket in the mail, and thinking it was for Austin, Kay and I went ballistic. We were afraid for Austin's safety and concerned that this could lead to the loss of his license one day. We came down hard on him to make sure he got the point. It turned out, however, that the ticket was for his sister Allison, who was away at college and wasn't there to fess up. I don't know if our tirade ensured that he won't run yellow lights, but it does mean he avoids intersections with traffic cameras.

Life with Austin had shown me that even people with great knowledge and the best of intentions can hold us back if we let them. The director of special education hadn't wanted to keep Austin from achieving his fullest potential. Likewise, the experts who told Karen that people with autism could never succeed at jobs in the distribution center didn't want to cheat people with disabilities out of their big chance.

But they were realists. They knew the landscape. Maybe they

were so focused on all the ways we could fail that they just couldn't see the ways we might succeed.

They were speaking from past experience. And actually, they were right. What we wanted to do was impossible. And it would remain impossible until we did it.

Doubt and inertia are the status quo's best friends. They always say no to change, risk, and innovation.

CHAPTER 27

DON'T LET THE BIG
ONE GET AWAY

OUR REAL ESTATE TEAM, working under the code name Project Lincoln, began a quiet search for possible sites for the new distribution center. Having been through a similar process many times in previous searches, the team methodically evaluated sites in terms of suitability for construction, cost of land, and access to highways and labor force. They eventually narrowed down their search to three areas: Atlanta, Georgia; Chattanooga, Tennessee; and Anderson, South Carolina.

I visited the finalist sites with our team. It was a lot of driving, a lot of facts, and a lot of trying to visualize a huge building and parking lots on empty fields. After a long day, we arrived at the last location on the list: Anderson, South Carolina. It's difficult to pinpoint why exactly, but we knew right away there was something special about this place. Beyond our gut feeling, there was an advanced medical center, a number of national chains, a viable downtown business district, a major university, and new schools. I put Anderson on the top of my list.

Typically our team worked with local development boards to flesh out details when finalizing our decision. However, this project added an unusual criterion to the list: Was the community able to support the employment of people with disabilities?

We were going to find out. On a September morning in 2003, Dale Thompson, the executive director of the Anderson County Disabilities and Special Needs Board, got an unexpected call from the Anderson County Development Board. He was offered an invitation to meet with an unidentified Fortune 500 company known only as Project Lincoln.

Dale had worked with people with disabilities since the days when about all they were allowed to do was make pot holders. His job was to secure employment for some of the most neglected, spurned, and feared humans in the community—people who not so many years ago were locked away in the South Carolina State Hospital. If they weren't penned up by the state, they were kept at home so "normal" people wouldn't be embarrassed by seeing them.

Dale knew the facts and witnessed the tragedies. One out of every five Americans has some disability. Seven percent of Americans have mental limitations or illnesses that interfere with their daily functioning. Only 16 percent of people with a severe disability such as deafness, legal blindness, intellectual disability, autism, or an inability to walk are employed. Twenty-seven percent live under the poverty level, compared with 9 percent of people without disabilities.[1]

Dale celebrated each measly, part time, sub-minimum-wage job—and sometimes the celebration lasted longer than the job. Employers were more likely to duck around a corner when they saw him coming than to slap him on the back. It was nothing personal—their hearts were with him, but their pocketbooks couldn't accommodate his needs. Hardly anybody in the country wants to hire such individuals, and nobody knows that any better than Dale.

Many of Dale's clients had never been employed at all—ever, in any way. Some had parents who had coddled, babied, and protected them until they weren't equipped to perform real work. Some couldn't concentrate; others were so focused on one thing that they couldn't handle distractions. Some had temper tantrums, and others couldn't be bothered to care. Some wouldn't stay on their medications, while others took so many meds that they went through their days like zombies. Some were physically weak. Some were severely overweight. And hardly any of them would be able to get to and from work on their own, as 90 percent of them couldn't drive.

Don't let the prospect of difficulty stand in the way of the grand possibility.

These were the people we hoped to employ.

It was the first time Dale's agency had been called into an exploratory meeting with a prospective business, and he was excited about the opportunity. He packed his charts, reviewed his statistics, and polished his pitch. He felt ready. But he wasn't.

The offer Dale was about to receive was bigger than anything he'd dared dream. He found himself in the rare, happy, and frightening position of being made completely dizzy by good fortune. It was a call he'd waited thirty years to receive—a moment he'd remained sure would come despite thousands of dashed dreams and expectations in the past.

Specifically, we were looking to hire a large number of people with disabilities. We were offering the same terms and conditions for all our new hires. Individuals with disabilities would work alongside other employees and be paid the same wages—$14 an hour to start, with regular raises, including vacation time, sick leave, health benefits, and profit sharing. They would have the same opportunities for advancement as any other employee.

Dale had never entertained such an offer. This was simply something that wasn't done. Not by big, private, for-profit employers. Not as a regular policy. Not in any kind of numbers. Not ever. Perhaps the name Lincoln was a long-awaited herald, he hoped—a sign that emancipation might be coming for one of the last groups in America still waiting for full civil rights.

But if Dale had never imagined anything as big as what we were offering that day, he'd also never faced anything as daunting as what we were asking for. We wanted employees who could do physical, demanding work that required constant attention. On top of that, speed was essential. Anyone who couldn't keep up wouldn't be able to keep the job.

We expected the employees with disabilities to work the same shifts as other employees—day, evening, and late night. Absenteeism would not be tolerated, nor would tardy arrival. This meant that the employees would need reliable transportation.

Of all the hurdles set before those with disabilities, perhaps none is harder to surmount than that of transportation. But if Project Lincoln made good on its promise, people with disabilities could earn enough money to live like other people. They could afford to pay for transportation and homes of their own. They could go out on a Saturday night. They could have friends. They could fall in love. They could marry and have children. They could go to movies—dances, even. And they'd have something to dance about. We were dreaming big, but there's something about doing the impossible that becomes contagious.

When we told Dale we wanted 220 people who were ready, willing, and able to work, he was too savvy to show surprise, but he did turn a bit pale. He could give us ten. Maybe. Anderson County and the three counties adjoining couldn't supply the number of workers of the quality we demanded. But as he sat thinking through the difficulties, he remembered all those people he felt he had disappointed—those who had yearned for a job, those who had been desperate to earn a wage and had never gotten the chance. One by one, they filed invisibly into his mind and stood hidden in the shadows, waiting and hoping that this time he could deliver.

So Dale Thompson did what any thoughtful, prudent man faced with the chance of a lifetime would have done. He lied.

"No problem," he said. "We can do that."

The prospect of difficulty would not stand in the way of the grand possibility. The moment had presented itself to him.

Little did Dale know how important his response was. We'd talked to a lot of people, but nobody had stepped up to the plate the way he had. We had high expectations, and we needed a partner as passionate as we were. Now we had one.

Don't let fear stop you from going after the big one. Its pursuit can inspire you to do the miraculous.

CHAPTER 28

ESTHER'S LESSON

ONE SUMMER DAY, as I stood on the deck overlooking our backyard, I wrestled with my doubts. I was worried that we would fail, afraid that I had overpromised and would underdeliver, certain that I'd be written off as a dreamer and lose my credibility—perhaps even my job. What had I gotten myself and Walgreens into?

"I wonder if this will really work," I said as Kay joined me on the deck.

Kay is the spiritual ballast of our family. Her faith, founded in the bedrock of a Baptist church in Kentucky, has become a stabilizing force in her life over the years. Love and compassion form the foundation of her faith, and she leans on it to support our family in the deepest, most life-giving ways.

"Remember the biblical story of Esther?" she asked. One of Kay's gifts is to draw on Bible stories without sounding the least bit preachy or self-righteous.

She reminded me that Esther was the Jewish wife of a Persian king who had been persuaded that all the Jews in Persia were a threat to his empire. When he ordered their execution, Esther was asked to intercede for her people. Although she was the queen, she knew that approaching the king without permission could be considered an affront and result in her own execution. She was afraid, and she shared her fears with her relative Mordecai, who told her, "Perhaps you were made queen for just such a time as this." Esther overcame her fears, and the Jews were saved. After Kay recounted the story, there was a long silence.

She looked at me and said quietly, "Perhaps you were made vice president for such a time as this." Then, with absolute conviction in her voice, she said, "All the angels and the powers of heaven are standing behind you."

> **Perhaps you were made for such a time as this.**

If we were to stop now, what would happen to all those people who were waiting for a chance to prove what they could do? The jobs we were offering would be more than just a paycheck. They would mean the chance to have a life. Nobody knew that better than Kay and I did. What would happen to all those parents who were wondering how their children would survive after they were gone?

I knew that this would be the regret of a lifetime if I let the opportunity pass and it turned out to be the only chance I got. If I were to stand before my Maker one day, what would I say? "I'm sorry, God. You gave me the chance, and I wanted to do it. I could have done it. I would have done it. But I was afraid to fail and lose my position and prestige, afraid that I might look stupid."

So I didn't stop.

Forget about losing face. Worry about what will happen if you don't have the courage to keep going.

CHAPTER 29

THE WORLD IS WAITING

ALTHOUGH WE DIDN'T publicize our efforts, word began to spread in the disability community about what we were attempting. People from across the country called and wrote to encourage us and thank us for what we were doing. Many letters were from parents or grandparents who shared their stories about family members with disabilities. They wrote of their disappointments, their struggles, their dreams of a future for their loved ones.

And they wrote about their love. Each letter was a reminder of both the great need and our ability to have a positive impact on the world. I posted each letter on giant bulletin boards in the corporate team work area so team members could see how important our endeavor was.

When people write to a company, it's like putting a note in a bottle and dropping it in the ocean. Many times they never know if anyone even reads it. They may get a form letter in reply or no response at all. But this was different. I answered every letter. I took the time to respond because I wanted people to know there was someone else on the other end. As I replied, I envisioned myself in the writers' shoes. Many of their stories broke my heart. And each letter I wrote steeled my resolve.

One of the parents we heard from was Desiree Neff. She and her son, Troy Mayben, lived in San Diego, but when a relative told them of a TV news report about our center, they packed their belongings and headed across the country to South Carolina. Even though the distribution center was two years away from opening, Desiree told Troy they would get by until Walgreens started hiring. And they'd be first in line for jobs.

Troy, who is legally blind, has a ferocious work ethic. He started working in a gas station on his sixteenth birthday. Over the follow-ing decade, he talked his way into better jobs, only to be fired when his employers realized he couldn't see well enough to work at a com-puter or a cash register.

This is your chance. You can't afford to fail.

Desiree, who has a rare muscle disease that occasionally requires her to use a walker, struggled to make a living wage. Once, while she was employed at a temporary hiring agency, she was sent to a client's business. The employer eyed the walker suspiciously, so Desiree told him that she only had to use it sometimes.

"That's good," he said. "Come back when you aren't using it."

At the new distribution center, there would be no need for cover-up, no need for apologies.

Before the construction for our center even started, Dale Thompson began canvassing the counties surrounding Anderson for workers. Each time he talked to a job counselor, he said, "Send us your best. This is our chance. We can't afford to fail."

Desiree and Troy had put their futures on the line for this dream. We had to make sure those jobs would arrive at the right time.

The world is waiting for the good you will do. Give the world your best.

CHAPTER 30

KATRINA

On August 29, 2005, the same summer we began construction on the Anderson distribution center, Katrina made landfall in New Orleans. Although there had been much discussion about the city's vulnerability to hurricanes and the possibility that it could be enveloped in a bowl of toxic waters, the city was unprepared. At first we breathed a sense of relief as the eye passed over the city and its levees held, but the respite was short. Katrina continued inland, bringing more torrential rains and flooding that breeched the levees. It was the worst civil engineering disaster in United States history. Floodwaters poured into the city, leaving much of it underwater for more than a month.

New Orleans was one of our company's key cities in the South, with more than fifty stores. In an instant, these stores vanished off the grid. We didn't know if our employees were safe or where they were. In the coming months, we learned they had been forced to relocate to cities across the country. We didn't know if the stores had been closed before people evacuated and whether cash registers had been left open or closed.

One night the prominent Walgreens store on Canal Street was featured on the national news. People waded in and out, taking whatever merchandise they could carry. A police officer, knee deep in the swirling water, shouted, "Stay calm! Take what you need and move on."

As the tragedy played out, I was with a group of distribution center managers in Dallas. We watched scene after scene on the news. The desperation of the residents was palpable. They needed help and medicine and basic supplies just to survive. Frustrated by the slow pace of the rescue effort, we thought we could do better. Walgreens had always been a company that rises to a challenge, especially in times of emergency, but we had to admit the magnitude of the damage and the need from Katrina was unprecedented.

Once we decided as a company to assist our fellow citizens in New Orleans, we started facing some formidable obstacles. While we had supplies in our distribution centers, we had no stores and no way to communicate with our employees in the city. Law and order was tenuous at best. Temporary trailers, which were necessary for mobile pharmacies, were nonexistent. Finally we located about 150 RVs in Toronto. We flew pharmacists from Boston and Detroit to Toronto, where they spent the weekend learning how to secure and drive the RVs. That Monday morning, they headed toward New Orleans, switching drivers so they could stay on the move. They stopped by our Perrysburg, Ohio, distribution center to load up with the needed supplies for the city.

In preparation for meeting the convoy at our distribution center, I flew to Perrysburg, where our team members waited to fill the RVs with the basic supplies that were most necessary for people who had lost everything. We worked all day to be ready when the convoy arrived. It rolled in after midnight, looking like the final scene of *Field of Dreams*, when hundreds of car headlights converged to set the baseball diamond aglow. One after another, RVs pulled into the dock area, where our team members descended with the speed and coordination of an Indy pit crew to load diapers, first-aid supplies, batteries, candles, canned food, and bottled water. As soon as one RV was loaded, the next would take its place.

Walgreens hired Chicago-area sheriff deputies to meet the caravan in New Orleans for added security. We set up makeshift pharmacies, staffing them with employees from all over the country who volunteered to help. Our plan was simple: give everything away to those who were in need.

Providing necessary medications in a disaster area was even more complicated than we'd imagined. Without a way to link to our national computer systems, pharmacists had no records to rely on.

> **This was not the time for standard operating policy; it was the time to do the right thing.**

The disoriented victims frequently couldn't remember the names of their medications, and the storm had washed away or destroyed their old prescription vials and bottles. In those cases, our pharmacists were forced to rely on the patients' description of illness and/or their memory of the pill's appearance. This was not the time for standard operating policy; it was the time to do the right thing. When people could not pay, we gave them their medicine anyway. For weeks following the disaster, we expanded this emergency pharmacy policy to cover Katrina's victims wherever they turned up.

Walgreens also took care of our employees who had been victims of the storm. Once we located them and ensured that they were safe, our local district manager disbursed money as needed from our employee benefit fund, avoiding the red tape that usually accompanies the approval process. We continued their pay until they were resettled and guaranteed them jobs in the cities they relocated to—some as far away as California and Tennessee.

In meeting the need, we realized that we might be punished by state pharmacy boards for going around standard protocols. We recognized the potential financial losses if employees took advantage of the situation by gathering paychecks without returning to work. We knew some employees might make up stories about their needs, exhausting the employee benefit fund and leaving others without assistance. We knew the risks, but it was the right thing to do in the circumstances, and we trusted our employees. We were not disappointed.

When a crisis hits, stay true to your values and do the right thing.

MANAGE IN THE GRAY

WHEN IT CAME time to pick a manager for Anderson, I selected Keith Scarbrough from the Perrysburg distribution center. With his experience overseeing the enclaves there, he recognized that people with disabilities could be exceptional employees. I also chose him for his equanimity and his determination to do the right thing even when exceptions to the rules needed to be made to accomplish our goals.

I would not have made that decision years earlier, when we began working together. Back then, I considered Keith a hard-nosed, bottom-line type of guy who allowed his desire for consistency to override compassion or extenuating circumstances. But he'd learned a few things over the years—and perhaps even more to the point, so had I.

Several years ago we had endured a spate of bad accidents in our distribution centers because people frequently ignored safety rules. As a result, I directed that anyone who violated safety rules would be fired on the spot. No exceptions.

Shortly thereafter, a popular team member who was on break

stepped onto a conveyor line to reach her water bottle. Keith fired her even though the line wasn't running and she had a firm grip, with little risk of an accident. But stepping on a conveyor belt is against our safety rules, and I had clearly stated the no-exceptions policy.

The team members believed Keith had unfairly fired the employee. Grumbling and discontentment spread, and some employees launched a campaign to unionize the plant. I realized that my no-exceptions policy ignored a reality of modern management—the need to manage in the gray areas. Few things are black and white, and good managers need to distinguish between the letter of the law and its intent. In my frustration with the recurring accidents, I had overreacted, leaving Keith little choice but to fire the employee in compliance with my directive.

> **While consistency is important for managing things like outcomes, processes, and products, it doesn't work as well when it comes to people.**

All organizations need a degree of consistency in order to function. If everyone did his or her own thing, chaos would rule. Employee relations and legal departments like consistency because it's easy to defend in the event of a lawsuit. Managers like consistency because rules promote stability and make it easier to regulate compliance. It avoids the "slippery slope" of making exceptions and takes the guesswork out of knowing where to draw the line.

Just as fear may be confused with respect, consistency is often confused with fairness. While consistency is important for managing things such as outcomes, processes, and products, it doesn't work as well when it comes to people. Ultimately, fairness matters more than consistency. And fairness requires judgment.

Applying judgment requires more skill and thoughtfulness than merely administering the rules. It requires considering the circumstances of each situation, our values, and what we want to achieve. My experience has been that judgment pays off in increased employee engagement and more responsive, thoughtful managers. Over the years, I have asked various groups of employees what type of work environment they would prefer to work in. Offered the choice of being governed by ironclad, no-exceptions rules or being governed by values, almost all prefer the latter.

In the weeks that followed the conveyor belt incident, Keith and the other managers worked to ensure that fairness and compassion tempered their enthusiasm for consistency. Keith recognized that he could be rigid at times and that his tendency to insist on doing things a certain way sometimes interfered with accomplishing the end objective. Over the months that followed, he became more flexible and more willing to listen to others when making a decision. His openness fostered renewed respect and understanding with the Perrysburg team members, and they began to trust each other again.

I knew that Keith's strength and compassion would be needed in light of the obstacles we were bound to encounter in Anderson. As we'd learned in Perrysburg, we needed to manage on a continuum, with consistency on one end and compassion on the other. Knowing that mistakes were inevitable, we determined to favor the side of compassion. Our motto for Anderson managers became "Consistent in objective, flexible in method." We were learning, in other words, to manage in the gray.

Fair is not always black and white. Good managers make calls based on intent, not the letter of the law.

CHAPTER 32

SHARE THE LOAD

GROWING UP IN TEXAS, I used to hear people say that the body beside the road with the arrows protruding from its back was the scout. When a victory is gained, the people out in front are often overlooked and unacknowleged. But without them, we could never reach our goals.

Building a modern distribution center is a huge undertaking. It involves constructing a ten-story building the size of fifteen football fields, with miles of conveyor to move everything from aspirin bottles to merchandise displays weighing a hundred pounds or more. Our distribution centers could barely handle the growing demands of existing Walgreens stores, not taking into account the new stores that were being constructed. Our schedule was tighter than the proverbial Las Vegas slot machine. In the meantime, we had to find, hire, and train more than two hundred people to operate complex and potentially dangerous machinery in order to be ready the day our doors opened.

Without the right scout, we might not have overcome the obstacles of ignorance, red tape, and inertia that hinder every big undertaking. Thankfully, though, Dale Thompson was our scout, our guardian, and our guide.

Business is all about customers, product, and profit. It's designed not to take care of people but to offer people the chance to take care of themselves. If people with disabilities are to assume their rightful position as full citizens in the workplace, they need to grapple with the demands of business. They have to succeed at jobs like the ones we were offering—jobs with high pressure, high expectations, rigorous cross-training, and the very real possibility of being fired. Dale knew that some social workers excused poor performance due to disability, but business would not. He also knew that every Walgreens team member would have to carry his or her load, disability or not.

Working in the new distribution center was a significant opportunity for some of these potential new hires—perhaps the only one that would appear for years. It was their chance to prove themselves as equals to other workers in the United States. Dale understood the system and the challenges to be overcome better than any of us at Walgreens ever could. We needed to stop speeding bullets and leap tall buildings in a single bound; Dale knew how.

For starters, the transportation problems seemed insurmountable. Our new facility was planned for a location on the outskirts of town with highway access for our trucks and sufficient space to accommodate such a large building. Surrounded by farmland and vacant fields, it wasn't accessible by public transportation, and the city had no plans to add routes to the area. And based on the research we'd done about the people in our hoped-for workforce, most of them lacked the income to own and maintain a car—and they wouldn't be able to drive even if they had one.

Since Walgreens was fully committed to the project, our government relations department proposed that the company donate

$100,000 to the city to cover the needed buses and new routes to move workers to and from the plant.

Reluctantly, I opposed the donation. The company had already taken huge steps to prove that people with disabilities could be productive workers, valued team members, and contributing representatives of their community. I believed that giving Anderson money would deny the community a chance to step up and be a part of the distribution center's success.

Dale and I talked it over, and he agreed. With the help of local business and civic leaders, he and Anderson-area state legislators convinced the South Carolina legislature to provide the city with $200,000 to purchase buses and establish the new routes.

With one problem solved, we barely had time to catch our breath before the issue of training arose. Our new employees needed to hit the ground running when the new facility opened, but there were no sites available for training. Dale came to the rescue again. With the assistance of the local economic development office as

When a victory is gained, the people out in front are often overlooked and unacknowledged. But without them, we could never reach our goals.

well as state and local officials, Dale secured another $300,000 in funds to establish mock workstations in a vacant building near his office. Walgreens supplied the machines, the state of South Carolina supplied the building, and state agencies supplied the trainers. We opened the training center with all the mock workstations up and running almost a year before the distribution center was scheduled to open.

Some people trained for a full year without pay in hopes of landing a spot on the Walgreens team. Other potential employees started exercise programs to increase their endurance and strength before they began full training for the jobs they desperately wanted. After the distribution center opened, we installed a training facility on site, setting up a practice area where people with disabilities could train for a few weeks or months at a time, until they were job ready. That facility remains in use five years later and is largely managed by our community partners to evaluate potential candidates.

The opportunity to work full time for full pay—with no distinction between workers with disabilities and those without—was both inspiring and frightening. Although most candidates had never made the kind of wages we were paying, parents had to be reassured that their children would be able to go back on Social Security payments if they took a job and lost it. Such an influx of income could create issues with some parents who were accustomed to controlling what little money their children earned through work or assistance. Dale and his team anticipated the problems and were ready with counseling—both therapeutic and economic.

When Dale had originally said yes to our proposal, he had no idea how it would be achieved, nor did he have the resources to ensure its success. The power and possibility of the idea had brought others on board. The community was no longer watching on the sidelines; the community was now engaged as part of the team.

Give others a chance to put skin into the game so they get the satisfaction of being part of the team and owning its success.

CHAPTER 33

SACAGAWEAS

THE STORY OF Anderson is about more than a big corporation doing charity work or a company deciding to do the right thing. It offers the lesson that every person—regardless of hardship, disability, and prejudice—can excel if given the opportunity. The distribution center in Anderson is a testimony that dreams do come true, that power and goodness are not contradictory.

When we began our project, no one understood the challenges we would face or how many people would contribute to our success. In many ways, we were like the nineteenth-century explorers Meriwether Lewis and William Clark, who were charged by President Jefferson with finding the "most direct and practical water communication across this continent." Without the help of various people along the way, especially a French-Canadian fur trapper named Toussaint Charbonneau and his young Shoshone wife, Sacagawea, it is unlikely the expedition would have succeeded.

So it was for us. Whenever we hit a roadblock—a problem that seemed irresolvable—a Sacagawea always appeared to guide us past obstacles and help us find a way to continue. Time and time again, challenges brought out the best in us.

One of those guides was Angie Campbell, who has cerebral palsy and whose grandfather had suffered with the same crippling malady. At six months, she wasn't crawling; she couldn't even hold up her head. Her hip socket was too small for the bone in her leg, and the heel cords in her legs weren't long enough for her to walk unless she was on her tiptoes. She was just eight months old when she had the first of many surgeries. From kindergarten through second grade, Angie was in special classes apart from the other children, even during lunch and recess. Sometimes, as she walked through the halls delivering a message from her classroom to the office, she looked in at the other classes, where everyone seemed much happier, and yearned to be among them.

Don't see others for what they can't do; see them for what they can do.

Angie was in the third grade when schools were required to mainstream students with disabilities. But being separated from the other students had put her behind in her studies, and because she couldn't write with a pencil, she was at an added disadvantage. At home she used a typewriter and would start on her homework right after dinner, usually working until ten o'clock. Though her body had limitations, her mind and will were strong.

Her grandfather, who had never been able to find work due to his disability, constantly encouraged her. "Don't let people tell you what you can't do," he said. "You'll find that out yourself. Listen to the ones who tell you what you can do."

As Angie advanced in school, often in accelerated classes, teachers put her in the back of the class and wouldn't allow other students to help her with the work. When she was in junior high, a math teacher failed her because she couldn't write straight columns of numbers. Understanding her struggles with writing, her parents asked if she could do her work orally or be given more time or fewer problems.

The teacher said, "If she's going to cut it in a normal class, she's going to have to do things like everyone else."

Angie's mother, Marlene, often showed up at school, cajoling teachers to give Angie a fair chance. Other members of the Campbell family might do fine without college, but education was Angie's only hope. Fortunately, she got a break that changed her life: she met a principal who cared.

"In four years, I'm going to Clemson University," Angie told him one day. "And I can't do that if I'm in a basic class."

"I believe you will be at Clemson, and we're going to help you do it," he said.

The principal got Angie a computer to use in class and made sure she wasn't relegated to the back of the room. She excelled, making straight As. And she refused to let her disability control her life. Angie ran for class president, delivering a speech before the entire school body. She entered the school beauty pageant, went to the Bahamas with her classmates, and learned to drive. And just as she'd promised, she went to Clemson, again making straight As and eventually graduating with a master's degree.

Eager to get a job, Angie sent out 250 résumés and went on sixty-five interviews. When she walked in and managers realized that she had cerebral palsy, she was turned down all sixty-five times.

"All people see is my disability," she says. "They see what I can't do, not what I can do."

She didn't stop trying to get work, finally applying for a job with the state agency in charge of securing employment for people with disabilities. When the interviewers there seemed hesitant about hiring her, she reminded them that (1) she was qualified and (2) it was illegal to discriminate against people with disabilities. She was hired.

I met this Sacagawea on one of my visits to the Anderson disabilities agency. As I left the office, Angie stopped me. "If there's anything I can do to help you, just let me know."

We sent her a job description for a position recruiting and managing people with disabilities at the new facility. When she read the Walgreens job description, she knew she was qualified on every count and began thinking she might find a place for herself there. Even though it had taken so much effort to get her current job, Angie couldn't let go of the idea.

"I like to define what I'm capable of for myself," she says. "I'm not going to let someone else tell me what I can do." Privately, she thought, *This may work or it may not work, but I want to be part of it.*

Angie's interview with us lasted two hours. Keith Scarbrough and his human resources manager, Larry Kraemer, grilled her while our disability consultant, James Emmett, listened in and questioned her by phone. While she had no problem answering their questions, they couldn't always answer hers. They needed someone to do something unprecedented. There were a lot of blanks that hadn't been filled in yet.

"How do you expect this person to do everything you're asking?" she asked.

They held their hands out, palms up. "We don't know."

"How many people will you hire?"

Again: "We don't know."

A day later, we offered her the job.

Angie needed two assistants who would serve as job coaches for the entire plant. These managers would work with all employees, whether they had a disability or not. They would act as liaisons between managers and workers—smoothing the way, creating opportunities, and offering guidance to anyone who needed it. There were no models for such positions. Angie already knew that she and her job coaches must be more than advocates and defenders of a special population. If employees with disabilities were going to be fully integrated into the workplace, then she and the job coaches would need to be resources for the managers as well as for the line workers.

It turned out that other people in unlikely places and circumstances were being prepared to help. They would join us at just the right time in the journey.

Ben Kelly, another Clemson graduate, was Angie's first hire. Ben was born with a congenital disorder that had caused him considerable inconvenience throughout his life. His feet were turned backward, and his fingers were bent toward his forearms. His arms were not only unusually short and without elbows, but they also lacked the muscles that would allow him to raise them above his shoulders. A string of surgeries, starting when he was an infant, turned his feet forward and made him look more like other children, but no one expected that he'd ever be able to walk. He wasn't even able to crawl properly. The doctors fitted him with a heavy set of leg braces, and he clumped around in them until he was eleven, when he built up enough strength and balance to wear regular shoes. Today he walks without even a hitch.

Doctors also tried to fix the muscles in Ben's arms, but that operation was unsuccessful. Since one of his arms was pretty much useless, he learned to pick things up using his good arm and his back and chest muscles. His fingers don't have much functionality either, but he makes the most of them.

No one could teach Ben how to do anything. Not because he wasn't willing to learn, but because he couldn't do anything the way others did it. Nobody else was like him. He was an adult before he met another person with the same disorder, and even that man's disabilities were different from his. But what Ben had going for him was an indomitable will. His mother always said that anytime someone told Ben he couldn't do something, he wouldn't quit until he proved the person wrong.

Like Angie, Ben couldn't find a job and was forced to spend three years living on disability assistance. Even Goodwill couldn't find anything for him at first. But the manager remembered him, and when some money came through to start a jobs program for people on parole, she hired him to set it up. Ben mentioned that a man who hadn't been able to get himself a job in three years of looking might not be the best choice to help others find work, but the manager said, "You already know every avenue there is for getting a job." Ben loved the job and thought he'd found his calling.

When he read a newspaper story about our new distribution center, he contacted our local office and offered to help us fill positions with his clients. Angie Campbell responded by visiting him at Goodwill.

After Angie left, Ben's boss said, "Now don't you be running out in the parking lot trying to get a job with Walgreens."

Angie had mentioned that she was looking for trainers to work with people with disabilities and to help as coaches for the staff and managers, so Ben watched an online video of a talk I'd given about what we hoped to do with our new distribution center. The next day Ben called Angie. Too shy to ask outright for the position, he joked around a bit, then said, "I guess since you've met me, you might take a look at my résumé if I send it over."

Angie doesn't joke about such matters. "Send it," she said. She hired him.

Mary Jones was her second hire for a job coach. Mary, a trainer who worked for Dale Thompson in enclaves and sheltered workshops, didn't have the educational background of the other trainers. But she brought the mothering skills of nurturing and patience—the result of raising two sons and growing up with a brother who has an intellectual disability. More important, she brought a strong set of expectations for her clients. She felt that other job coaches sometimes expected too little and were content to let the clients set their own achievement levels. Mary had seen the results of such attitudes. But while she was demanding, she was also kind. She would go the extra mile to help her clients even as she expected them to help themselves.

When Mary heard about what we were doing at Walgreens, she called and e-mailed everyone she knew in the disability employment field to let them know that this was the chance of a lifetime for their clients.

Her job title may be job coach, but ultimately Mary is the warehouse mama. She chides and praises and gently steers everyone—from the managers to the truck loaders—into being the kind of people they really want to be. She is willing to do whatever it takes to help people succeed. If that means setting challenges, she'll do it. If it means offering rewards and praise, she'll do that, too. Mary's standards are high, and she doesn't accept excuses.

With the balance of Ben, the process-oriented guy who can find a work-around for any kind of problem, and Mary, the at-work mom who expects and receives the very best work from people, Angie has just the balance she needs.

Keep your eyes open for strangers who are being prepared to help you.

CHAPTER 34

TOUGH LOVE

WE KNEW THE number one staffing challenge would be to find
people with disabilities who could do the work. Given the disappointments they had likely faced in the past, we also knew that
many potential employees had already given up and might not be
reachable through conventional channels. We did everything we
could think of to get the word out to applicants.

We took out ads in papers all over the surrounding area. We
hosted a job fair, working until dusk to serve the hundreds of
people who showed up.

Angie was looking for a sense of urgency among potential hires.
"This is a fast-paced place," she told recruiters. "Couch potatoes won't
make it. Attitude is everything." If people wanted to do the work, we
could make the accommodations needed for their disability.

As team members were being hired, Angie was also helping those
in management get prepared. Most had never worked with people
with disabilities and were anxious about it, even if they didn't openly
express their concerns. Keith Scarbrough would sit down with managers and supervisors at the end of the day and have them write their
concerns anonymously on slips of paper and then drop them into a

hat that was passed around. Keith would pull out one piece of paper at a time and discuss each issue until the hat was empty. He didn't always have the answers. He acknowledged that we would make mistakes along the way and that when we did, we would correct them and move on. He understood the power of honesty, and most often, that was assurance enough.

Richard Hall came from the South Carolina Vocational Rehabilitation Department to help recruit and train new hires. Several decades of work in the textile mills had taught Richard tough lessons about what it takes to make a factory run. Before the mills began closing, he'd risen from a line worker to a manager. By the time we came to town, Richard had reinvented himself as a production coordinator with the South Carolina Vocational Rehabilitation Department.

His tough pragmatism was a good balance to the social-work approach some of his colleagues had. Having heard countless promises and experienced almost as many disappointments during the tough days when the textile industry was moving overseas, he was cautious about believing that good intentions would result in good outcomes. He knew two things for sure: for any business plan to succeed, it had to have the support of top management. And it had to make money.

Our plan passed both tests, which made Richard hopeful. *Maybe,* he thought. *Maybe something big is around the corner.* If it was, he was ready to make it happen.

Angie holds everyone to a high standard, which sometimes means she needs to fire people. She ended up firing four of the candidates Richard recommended in the first few weeks. Some days she cried all the way home, feeling like the meanest woman on earth. But she was committed to the "same performance standards" rule, and she was tireless in applying it.

This is our chance, she told herself. *We have to make it.*

As far as I was concerned, Richard and Angie were both doing exactly what they should do. It was a painful task, but it was what we had to do if we were going to change the way people viewed those with disabilities in the workplace. The work in a distribution center isn't cut out for everyone—disability or no disability.

When people realized that some workers would fail despite our best efforts, they asked if we were being heartless to get those workers' hopes up only to have them dashed. In our view, the alternative was worse. We were giving individuals an opportunity

If we avoided the possibility of failure and the pain of firing someone, we would be denying a chance to those who might be successful.

they might not have had otherwise, and we, too, were disappointed when it didn't work out. But if we avoided the possibility of failure and the pain of firing someone, we would be denying a chance to those who might be successful. To do so would have been the greater sin in my eyes.

If we were to achieve the business goals that enabled us to consider this initiative in the first place, it was paramount that we insist on maintaining high performance standards for people with disabilities. What we didn't know at the time was that this commitment would transform our workplace culture—and eventually the entire division and company.

Denying people the chance to achieve because you're afraid they will fail is just another way of holding them back.

CHAPTER 35

FAILURE IS NOT AN OPTION

In June of 2007, operations began. The machines cranked up just as planned. All the employees knew their jobs. Orders were filled, trucks were loaded, and we started shipping to stores. Job counselors from the community who had worked alongside employees in the mock workshops went on the line with them in the factory.

Some people had trouble transitioning. For starters, they had to adjust to the noise of the machinery and to changes in workflow. If they were expecting twelve items and they got fourteen instead, some of them would become confused. If the line backed up and there was nothing to do, they had to learn to wait. But as we'd already found, anything that could be explained in simple steps could be taught. The employees with disabilities coped better than all the doubters thought they would. Once they fastened on to the work, most had laser-like focus. Not only did they work hard; they didn't want to quit.

Our grand experiment was looking good. Then we cranked things up a notch, and the chaos began.

In an automated building, everything works together and is mutually interdependent. When it works, it's a thing of beauty, but when something stops in one area, all other areas are affected. We had lots of breakdowns. Sometimes we had wrong data; other times we had wrong items, wrong counts, or delays in deliveries.

As problems surfaced, we solved them and got things back on track. Then we'd add more stores, and the stress would cause another area to break down. Deliveries would be late. Orders would be filled incorrectly. Store managers began to complain—and rightfully so; they had customers to serve. As the retail saying goes, "Never forget where the cash registers are."

In a chain like Walgreens, when an item that should be on the store shelf isn't there, we lose more than just one sale. Almost half of our sales are impulse items—a customer comes in looking for one thing and buys another unplanned item on the way out. If customers don't find an item they're looking for, we're likely to lose the sale of two items, not just the one thing they came in for. Every second's delay in the operation of a distribution center means lost profit. In a business that plots the difference between success and failure by one-eighth of a penny, loss shows up quickly and can be disastrous.

> **We had to face the brutal facts of the situation and keep moving forward.**

To the stores, it looked as if we didn't know what we were doing. Things would get better and then get worse, and the cycle kept repeating as we added more volume. Slowing things down would have only spread the disruptions over a longer period.

However appealing a slowdown might have sounded, the long-term financial impact and customer disruption would have likely been worse.

One of my favorite movies is *Apollo 13*, which tells the story of the failed mission to the moon in 1970. Gene Krantz, the NASA flight director, is a key character. When circumstances start to look dire and the flight team in Houston tells him it's unlikely they will be able to return the three astronauts to Earth safely, Krantz replies resolutely, "Failure is not an option!" In our own way, we were at the same point. Failure was not an option.

We couldn't turn back. We had to face the brutal facts of the situation and keep moving forward, making sure we were doing everything we could to identify problems and get them fixed in short order.

Everyone on the team—especially those in the IT and engineering divisions who had designed the systems—knew we were letting the stores down and worried that some people would lose patience or think we'd overreached in our goals. Many expressed concern that they were letting me down too. I reassured them of my faith in them, lest they lose faith in themselves. I'd never seen anyone do their best work under fearful circumstances. And the situation demanded everyone's best.

Whenever times were dark, I would remind them of another Gene Krantz line from *Apollo 13*: when the director of NASA tells Krantz that this mission could be the worst disaster in the history of the space program, Krantz replies, "With all due respect, sir, I believe this is going to be our finest hour." I believed it could be our finest hour as well, whether anyone recognized it or not. Win or lose, we would press on.

When things get desperate, keep pressing on. This just may be your finest hour.

CHAPTER 36

BREATHING LIFE INTO THE DREAM

BEFORE THE INITIAL launch of operations, we had gathered all the team members together to celebrate the kickoff. With the entire workforce assembled for the first time, I thanked them for what they were about to do. I reminded them that they were part of a long-standing dream that had begun years earlier and that this moment marked the culmination of so many hopes. Their accomplishments would be the breath that would bring the dream to life.

Now, with operations at full tilt, everyone at the Anderson distribution center knew what was at stake. They were determined not to let one another down, and they didn't. Although no one in the stores or at corporate ever said that the problems we were having might be attributed to the fact that we'd hired people with disabilities, I wondered if that was in the back of people's minds. Those of us close to the work knew better. The team on the floor was pouring it on, coming in every Saturday and working overtime every day. Any worries we'd had about individuals with disabilities not being flexible, not being strong enough to work extra hours, and not being able to get transportation to work were thrown out the window. The people at the Anderson plant definitely weren't the problem. The team members were working together better than I'd ever seen a distribution center crew work.

After about four months of fits and starts, fatigue was setting in. I knew it was time for a morale-boosting visit to Anderson. Having been through this before with other start-ups, I expected two questions: "When are we going to get a Saturday off?" and "When are you going to get this equipment working?" But this was no ordinary distribution center. No one brought up the questions I'd expected. Instead, employees asked, "How are we doing?" Hmm, that was a first. And then came the clincher: "What can we do to help?"

They had not given up. Despite their personal sacrifices, they weren't thinking of themselves and the toll that the long hours were taking. They weren't looking for someone to blame for all the problems. They were focusing on making the dream come true.

I'd known all along that the culture in this distribution center would be different from anything we'd ever experienced. I just hadn't known exactly what kind of different. I had gone down to boost their morale. Instead, they boosted mine.

Operations began to smooth out as the kinks were gradually worked out of the systems. Now Anderson had to prove itself in everyday operations. They were up to the challenge, though— those Anderson team members wouldn't complain and wouldn't quit, no matter how hard the job got.

Among those employees were Desiree and Troy, the mother and son who had come to Anderson from California two years earlier. Now Desiree could use her cane or her walker whenever she needed it. Troy no longer had to hide his visual deficits, and he was able to use the computers because they were set up with symbols large enough for him to see.

Troy and Desiree weren't at the distribution center long before they befriended twenty-four-year-old Brittany Heydrich, who has a developmental disability and has difficulty speaking because of a stutter and aphasia. Eventually Troy and Brittany fell in love and got married. This couple, who had always lived with their parents, bought a car and their own condo. "She's my eyes, and I'm her voice," says Troy of his wife.

Also on the team was Derrill Perry, a forty-nine-year-old man with a developmental disability, who had been employed in a work-

The reality turned out to be far greater than the dream.

shop where he was paid less than a dollar an hour. When Derrill first came to work at the distribution center, he walked with his head down and his eyes on the floor, rarely saying anything to anybody. On the day he earned his first Walgreens paycheck, he handed it to his mother, and she began to cry. He used part of that paycheck to treat his parents to a dinner out—his first time to pay the bill in a restaurant. The next day, he asked his supervisor, Rico Robinson, "Why did my mother cry?"

"I don't know," Rico replied. But he knew. And as Rico now says, we all knew.

Derrill and his parents attended the open house held shortly after the center opened. With his mother walking beside him, Derrill pushed his father's wheelchair. When I reached out to shake Derrill's dad's hand, he pulled me in for a hug and whispered in my ear, "Thank you. My family is finally safe. Now I can die knowing they'll be all right." I had no reply. I just nodded and squeezed his hand in return.

Within a year, Derrill's father died. Derrill was the sole support for his mother—his salary more than either of his parents had ever earned.

Another member of the Anderson team, Jennifer, has bipolar disorder, and she can cycle quickly from one extreme to another. She might be fine one moment, but the next she can suddenly become paranoid and begin cursing at everyone, including her boss. No matter her state, however, her accuracy and speed never falter. On her bad days, the coaches encourage her to take a break, put her feelings in a journal, and listen to music.

"Even on her bad days, she still outperforms everybody else," Angie says. "But she needs more understanding. We try to help her decompress. She just wants to be heard."

Jimmy, a young man with autism, is quick and flawless in his work. He works with precision, steady and untiring.

His coworker Terry, who is mute, wins all sorts of performance awards that the management team has devised. Because he loves barbecue, his awards are often accompanied by a free meal at a local barbecue restaurant. He has figured ways to communicate without speaking, either through gestures or writing. Every day when his supervisor comes in, Terry wants to know, "How many are we going to do?" If she says, "Eight hundred," he promises, "I'm going to do a thousand."

One employee nicknamed Little Mama routinely performs at 110 percent of standard. She says she can do 120 percent but it makes her tired.

Billy, who reads at the third-grade level, loves unicorns, so his workstation is identified by pictures of unicorns. Other team members who love race cars might be given a photo of a race car every day. If Ben, the job coach, learns that an employee loves a particular celebrity, he rewards him or her by Photoshopping a picture of the star with the team member's own face superimposed next to the celebrity.

There are, of course, occasional blips. Little Mama doesn't always stay on the work platform. Jennifer still sometimes cuts boxes toward herself instead of away. In group productivity meetings, David wouldn't stop talking about President Obama. So Angie put a diagram on the whiteboard with "Talk" on one side and "Listen" on the other. She then explained that when she pointed to "Talk," it was all right to speak. When she pointed to "Listen," everyone needed to listen. It worked. Come to think of it, that strategy could have been helpful at a few executive meetings I've attended.

Larry Campbell, Angie's dad, was so excited by what we were doing that he wanted to become part of it too. He left his job at a local hospital and came to work in maintenance at the distribution center. "I see people with disabilities just like my daddy had," he says. "They walk like my daddy and talk like my daddy, and they're in management."

Despite the four people Angie had to fire initially, 85 percent of the team members that Richard Hall helped place are still working for us seven years later—a much higher retention rate than we experience in our other centers among those without disabilities. Richard once told a group of visitors, "There are people who, two years ago, I would have put my hand on a Bible and said would never work. Now they're successful, contributing members of society."

Our gamble was paying off. People with disabilities were doing more than we'd ever expected. I'd hoped that they could meld into the workforce, make rate, work a full shift, and be accepted by the other team members. They did all that—and the story might have ended right there. But the reality turned out to be far greater than the dream.

Never underestimate the power of purpose and the belief that you can make a difference.

CHAPTER 37

POSITIVE DISTRACTIONS

I HADN'T FORGOTTEN my larger dream of employing people with disabilities throughout the division and the entire company. Everyone was excited about Anderson and what we had done. But Anderson had only six hundred employees; the division employed a total of about ten thousand people in our distribution centers. How could we build on the success of Anderson and expand the vision to other centers?

The next step was to bring all the distribution center managers to Anderson for our annual meeting. Habitat International, the carpet manufacturer that Karen Preston had discovered when we were looking for employers who hire a significant number of people with disabilities, is located in Chattanooga, only a few hours away from our center. I saw an opportunity to show the managers how well a company with little automation and a large percentage of people with disabilities could operate. We rented a bus and headed across the state line to see the operation firsthand.

Habitat owner David Morris likes to call disabilities "positive distractions." As he introduced employees on the factory floor,

Morris spoke about each person's disability in the same way he might mention someone's hair or eye color—without a trace of pity or condescension. He spoke of each team member with respect and deference, the way the best coaches acknowledge the contribution of a team member after a great play. He gave people the freedom to be themselves, with no need to hide their disabilities. His candor and authenticity were liberating.

Watching how seamlessly Morris included people with autism, I thought of Austin. Just after Anderson opened, our youngest, Allison, entered her senior year in high school. One day as we were discussing her plans for college, we talked about all the changes this would mean for everyone. Kay and I knew that she would be taking a piece of our hearts with her when she moved away to college. It would be a big adjustment for Austin, too.

Although Austin had just graduated from high school, he would remain in the school's transition program for a few more years.

"Austin is going to miss you too," I told Allison. "You're probably his best friend at school."

"No, Dad," she said. "I'm not his best friend. I'm his only friend."

My heart sank as she continued. "When Austin walks through the halls, the crowds part around him."

She was right. At Austin's high school graduation, as each graduate crossed the stage to receive his or her diploma, the boisterous cheers of friends and family rang out. Austin walked across the stage in silence but for the claps of his immediate family.

Exclusion was an ache that never healed. I had felt it on Austin's behalf. And the memory of the enclave experience in Waxahachie never left me.

I thought about how people tended to view Austin. They judged him; they saw his disabilities and dismissed him. Satisfied in their own sense of good fortune, they may have felt uncomfortable pity as he passed by.

But was I so different? When it comes to disabilities, my experience with Austin has certainly made me more sensitive. However, I, too, can be dismissive and judgmental. If I consider others at all, my first thoughts are usually of assessment. *Is this person a threat? How does he stack up against me? Is she smarter? Richer? Does he have more status? More power?*

My experience at Habitat that day had a significant impact on me personally as well as professionally. I saw myself with all my ego, all my selfishness, all my pettiness, all my fears. I saw the things I work so hard to keep hidden from others because I fear that if they knew how small-hearted I really am, they wouldn't want anything to do with me.

The workers at Habitat were men and women with obvious challenges. There was no hiding here. And there was no shame. David had it right: here a disability was just a distraction from the typical, not a flaw in a person's humanity. Brokenness was not a source of shame, nor were gifts a source of pride. There was no "worthiness" test. Results for the team were what mattered.

When I looked at the Habitat employees, I saw the better version of myself reflected back—a more open, grateful, generous, and helpful me. I saw the good parts of me that are there but have been suppressed by all the getting and spending, the search for status and security, and the worry about not having enough.

I no longer saw these individuals for their disabilities. I saw their strengths, and it was a source of strength for me. The better person in me—no longer strapped down by my faults—began to stir.

What would it be like if we had a workplace that revealed the better person inside each of us?

What would it be like if we had a workplace that revealed the better person inside each of us? A workplace where all members are seen as equals, each person with his or her views, struggles, and roles? A place where no one is more worthy than another, but each one is unique?

As we left Chattanooga, my mind was whirling. I wondered if the distribution center managers had seen what I had.

There is no "them"; there is just "us." Making that idea a reality changes the workplace. And the world.

CHAPTER 38

CLEAR AND ELEVATING GOALS

DURING A MEETING with distribution center managers in Green Bay a few months earlier, I'd held up two pieces of paper, one in each hand. One represented "where we are" in hiring people with disabilities, and the other represented "where we can be." I started with both hands low and told the managers that I would begin raising the "where we can be" paper. Their job was to start clapping when I'd gotten the pieces of paper an appropriate distance apart. As the "where we can be" paper moved higher and higher, there were a few claps. Finally, when I could go no farther, the room burst into applause. The enthusiasm was there, but the way forward was not yet clear. The other distribution centers didn't have the level of automation that had made it possible for us to launch the initiative on such a large scale at Anderson.

After we returned from Habitat, the excitement was palpable, but this time it was grounded in a tangible vision. We'd been given a real-life glimpse into what could be, and we were more eager than ever to take off.

Habitat had helped the managers from other distribution

centers see a future that they'd previously thought was impossible. They'd seen a competitive environment where people with disabilities were succeeding without the help of automation. David's company didn't have any cutting-edge equipment. He had learned the same lesson that Phil at Carolina Fine Snacks had learned and the lesson we ourselves had learned in Anderson: it's not about technology; it's about opening yourself to new ways of thinking. People, not technology, are what make success possible.

I was reminded of the tale about stone soup. The story begins when a stranger comes into the village asking for food. When nobody offers anything, he announces that he will prepare a wonderful meal of stone soup for the entire village if someone will loan him a large kettle. As a curious crowd gathers, he puts water and a stone into the kettle and sets it over a fire. Periodically he tastes the boiling water, proclaiming it perfect except for the lack of this or another vegetable. Each time, a villager volunteers the missing ingredient until the stranger proclaims the soup perfect, pulls out the rock, and serves it to the villagers.

The villagers had needed the stone there first to overcome their fears and pitch in to make the soup. We had developed the technology to create a more efficient center. But the technology had also been the stone that helped us conquer our own fears and believe that people with disabilities could be successful in a fast-paced, competitive environment.

It was time to pony up. Before the managers went back to their own distribution centers, I told them it was time for them to set a "clear and elevating" goal. By *clear*, I meant that the goal should be specific and easy to understand and that it should have a deadline. By *elevating*, I meant that the goal would fire our imaginations, inspire us to our best efforts, and be difficult but not impossible to achieve. As an example, I pointed to John F. Kennedy's bold proposal in 1961, just three weeks after the country's first manned space flight, which had lasted less than twenty minutes. He promised that the United States would safely land a man on the moon by the end of the decade. His clear and elevating goal was achieved on July 20, 1969, with 164 days to spare.

But I wasn't JFK, and the goal couldn't come from me. It had to be theirs. I asked what we could achieve in five years. After a bit of discussion, the managers set an employment goal that we'd have one thousand people with disabilities in our distribution centers by the end of the decade, almost five years away. In a workforce of ten thousand people, that translated to one out of every ten employees. It was an ambitious goal, to be sure, and something that had never been done before.

This was a mission with meaning, and meaning is a powerful motivator.

The goal was both clear and elevating, especially considering it came in addition to our already-established goal of increasing productivity every year.

The next task would usually be to lay out the incentives to encourage team members to work toward achieving the goal. But in my experience, when there is a desirable incentive, most people try to negotiate the lowest possible target, doing only what they have to do to reach the reward. At the other end of the spectrum, incentives can be paralyzing if they make people afraid of not achieving the goal. The fear of failure can get in the way of creativity, and we desperately needed creativity.

The detrimental effect of fear on creativity can be demonstrated in a famous problem-solving experiment called "Duncker's candle problem." Participants are given a cigar-size cardboard box, a book of matches, and a candle, and they are assigned the task of putting a lit candle on the wall without the wax dripping on the floor. One team is told they are to complete the task so technicians can learn how much time to allot for future groups to complete the same task in a similar setting. A second group is told that it's a contest and that the group that accomplishes the task most quickly will receive a financial reward. Surprisingly, group one consistently completes the task faster than group two, leading the researchers to conclude that the stress of "losing" and not getting a reward diminishes creativity and teamwork.

Walgreens distribution center managers were leaders with track records of success. They had a goal that would significantly benefit the community. This was a mission with meaning—a powerful motivator. They aimed high because they hadn't been given a reason to fear failure. No further incentives were needed.

As soon as word got back to corporate, concerns began to surface. How were we going to count? That is, how would we define a disability? Would everyone have to self-identify? What about those with disabilities we already employed? What if we published the goal but didn't make it? How would we hold people accountable? I felt like the pastor who, when asked if tithing should be 10 percent of gross or 10 percent of net, answered, "Either."

If we got close to a thousand, it would be astounding, no matter how we counted. The same was true for the deadline. A deadline would force us into action, and the accomplishment would be significant, whether we made it or not. To worry about negative consequences if we fell short would only get in the way of our larger goal. As for how we were going to hold people accountable, they were going to hold themselves accountable. The goal was clear: it had a specific target and timetable. The goal was elevating: it was meaningful work that would require our very best. And most important, it was *their* goal.

Set a clear and elevating goal that inspires and challenges. Focus on what can be, not on what can go wrong.

CHAPTER 39

VERILY, VERILY

WE WERE CONFIDENT that the distribution center managers would hold themselves accountable. But a few questions remained. How would we keep focused on the goal? How would we have a way to know if we were on track?

In my earlier days at Walgreens, I liked to bounce ideas off people. I found that sometimes, to my chagrin, they took a brainstorm as a directive and started implementing it. At the other extreme, sometimes I'd hint at something rather than issuing a specific instruction, in the hope that they'd pick up on the hint and make it their own. But this method was often ineffective. Then one morning the solution came from an unexpected source: Kay's Bible study sessions.

When she filled me in about that week's study at the breakfast table, as she occasionally does, I learned that there is no underscoring in Greek. So in the Bible, when Jesus says something important, it's preceded with the words "Verily, verily." I thought this was an ideal solution to my communication dilemma, so I shared it with everyone at work. When I wanted to make sure they knew I thought something was important, I would precede or end it with "verily, verily." It prevented a lot of misunderstandings.

Sometimes those words were sufficient. But in some matters, the "verily, verily" had to take the form of action.

I already had a great example to follow in Walgreens history. We had tripled the number of our stores in just the last few years of our one hundred–plus years in business. To do so, Walgreens had set clear and elevating goals: double our stores in the next ten years, and then double them again over the next ten years. We had a similar clear and elevating goal: have one thousand people with disabilities in our distribution centers by 2010. Check.

Cultural change does not happen overnight; it requires years of reinforcement.

But what had kept the store growth on track was a continuous focus on the goal and our progress in achieving it. No extra incentives or accountability measures were needed. The CEO talked about it. The president talked about it. All the officers talked about it. Everyone up and down the organization knew about it. And we tracked our progress constantly. We had dozens of measures to monitor the day-to-day business of running the drugstores, but there were only two measures posted on the electronic bulletin board in the cafeteria: the number of stores we operated and the number of stores we had opened year to date.

This situation was a little different. To achieve our goal of "one thousand by 2010," every distribution center would have to play its part, and each center was unique. Some centers were growing quickly and creating new openings that could be filled by people with disabilities. Other centers' workloads were growing slowly, if at all, which meant that hiring opportunities would have to come primarily from employee turnover.

Monitoring raw numbers worked for store growth, but we needed a more sensitive, site-specific standard than just counting total employees with disabilities or the number of new hires with disabilities each year. In light of the differences in opportunity among the various buildings, we settled on recording the percent of new hires with a disability at each site and division wide. This enabled us to compare the progress of individual centers despite differences in total hires, and it also allowed us to monitor the division's overall progress.

Early on, we figured that the number we needed to shoot for over the next five years was one in ten. However, we knew we wouldn't start out at that level, because the centers were starting from scratch. But the goal ensured that everyone had to get moving, because the clock was ticking. Each month we recalculated the needed percentage of projected new hires with disabilities to make our goal. If we fell behind, the number would rise.

Applying the verily, verily principle to ensure that everyone knew this wasn't just a "program of the month," I talked about our goals often, monitored our progress, and let people know how we were doing. I saw it as my job to remind them that this was still important and to make sure the goal didn't get lost in the milieu of other demands. We couldn't let this initiative become part of what is known in education as the null curriculum—that which is not discussed is not important.

It takes longer than you think to overcome history. Cultural change does not happen overnight; it requires years of reinforcement and constant attention. As every athlete knows, it takes more effort to stay in shape than it does to get in shape.

The status quo is like Whac-A-Mole: you have to keep whacking.

CHAPTER 40

BEING ANDREW

I MAY BE able to name more of Snow White's dwarfs than I can the twelve apostles, but not so with Kay. After she told me about Andrew, he became my favorite. Most everyone has heard of Peter; not as many know about Andrew. Andrew was Peter's brother, and according to Kay, he was among the first to hear Jesus preach. He went to his brother and said something along the lines of, "You gotta get a load of this guy!" If it hadn't been for Andrew, there might not have been a Saint Peter.

I love this story, because sometimes we are Peter, but more often we are Andrew. When it comes to doing something big, it's easy to say, "I'm not a high-powered exec. I don't have any authority." Okay, we may not always be Peter, but we can be Andrew. And there would be no Peters were it not for the Andrews of this world.

I loved telling executives from other companies that nothing would make us happier than to be their Andrew. We would be their biggest fans if they wanted to take our methods and use them as their own—or even better, improve upon them.

Greatness is proprietary, but goodness can be shared without being diminished.

The first step in being Andrew was telling what we'd seen. What was happening at Walgreens was bigger than any competitive issue; it was about how businesses could "do good" in both senses of the phrase. They could give dignity and citizenship to people who had been denied a place in the world *and* be better, more efficient, more profitable businesses at the same time.

Outside experts studied hundreds of thousands of hours of our performance data and published results in professional journals.[1] They confirmed our own findings: people with disabilities perform their jobs just as well as other workers. In addition, they aren't absent as much, and they don't have as high a turnover rate. With the steep costs associated with absenteeism and turnover, we more than make up for the accommodations that are required to hire these individuals. And since people with disabilities work more safely, workers' compensation costs are lower too. One surprising finding was that deaf forklift drivers, whom everybody had worried about initially, had substantially fewer accidents than drivers who could hear. In short, our decision made good business sense.

Walgreens had a long history of being closemouthed about how we did things—partly to avoid revealing secrets, but also because part of our basic Midwestern ethic is to let our actions speak for us. But once we knew that our disability initiative was successful and that it had the potential to make an impact on the entire workplace, we knew we couldn't keep it to ourselves. As word spread through the business community, I began to receive invitations from industry associations asking me to speak at their conferences. Everywhere I spoke, I invited companies to visit our distribution centers.

I told them that when it comes to disability hiring, "What's ours is yours." Some companies wanted to send their engineers to look at our systems. We told them not to come, because our success in hiring people with disabilities was not dependent on technology. If they wanted to visit, they should bring the operations people instead—the ones who run the place, do the hiring, and are responsible for results. If their operations team would spend a day with us, I promised we would rock their world. I told them we call it the "Yes, Virginia, there is a Santa Claus" tour. Drawing on the hundreds of infomercials I'd seen, I even offered a money-back guarantee. Many companies took us up on the offer to visit, and none ever asked for a refund. I told the leaders of each company, "If you do this, we won't let you fail."

We conducted tours for leaders of dozens of other Fortune 500 companies as well as companies from around the world. One of the first things they saw was a large sign

Greatness is proprietary, but goodness can be shared without being diminished.

that had been inspired by my early visit to Waxahachie, when a team member in Waxahachie pointed out that although she was in the photo with the people with disabilities, she was not one of "them." The sign has the word *them* in the middle of a circle with a slash through it.

No *them*.

Just *us*.

If the visiting companies liked what they saw, we offered a workshop so their employees could get firsthand experience in an inclusive environment. At Anderson, we called it boot camp. Many companies—including Lowe's, Best Buy, Meijer, Procter & Gamble, Colgate, T.J.Maxx, Marks & Spencer in the UK, AT&T, and AutoZone—have launched their own initiatives.

Some people get it immediately. Steve Szilagyi, my counterpart at Lowe's, is one of them. When I met him at an industry conference, he said he had heard about us and wanted to visit. Knowing that Lowe's operations were different from ours, I was concerned that Steve would be put off by the level of automation we used. I warned him to not be sidetracked by the technology. Instead, I asked Steve to focus on how the people performed their jobs and interacted with one another. I asked him to call me after his visit so I could remind him that it wasn't about the equipment.

After the visit, he didn't even wait until he got back to his office. He called me from the car on his way to the airport. When I answered, the first words out of his mouth were, "I get it! And we want it!"

Lowe's quickly launched its own program from scratch. Within two years, Lowe's had more than three hundred people with disabilities in their distribution centers throughout the United States. On a visit to our center in Moreno Valley, California, I stopped by the nearby Lowe's distribution center unannounced and introduced myself. The site manager was delighted to see me and enthusiastically told me about Lowe's disability hiring and the positive impact it was having. He sounded exactly like our managers.

Why have power if you don't use it for good?

Jeri Swierzewski, head of distribution at Best Buy, saw what we were doing, and when she launched Best Buy's new e-commerce fulfillment center, she exceeded what we had achieved. Half of that center's workforce is composed of people with disabilities.

Even more surprising was Rick Keyes, head of manufacturing and logistics at Meijer, a respected general merchandise and grocery big box retailer in the Midwest. I met Rick after speaking at a conference and invited him to visit us. He said, "Thanks, but I heard you speak before, and it made sense. So we went back and started our own program."

Other visitors required a little more reflection. One CEO who was visiting our center with his team acknowledged that what we had done was impressive. He also proclaimed that he had the power to make this happen if he decided to back it. But if performance was the same, he argued, why should he go through all the effort it would take to hire people with disabilities? He'd heard the hard data about lower safety costs, higher retention, less absenteeism, and better teamwork. I could have reminded him of those benefits. Instead, I asked him a question that cut to the heart of the matter: "Why have power if you don't use it for good?" Clearly a person accustomed to having the last word, he nodded.

Almost every team that visited us left excited. But a lot can happen on the way back from the mountaintop to the valley. Sometimes the enthusiasm got lost in the shuffle of everyday demands back home. Memories dimmed and uncertainty grew as time passed. And we never heard back from them.

Every once in a while a team would visit and simply be unable to believe what they were seeing. No amount of data would persuade them.

And then there were those who came and saw something they'd only hoped to be true. They saw something that struck a chord deep within—that this was not just the smart thing to do, it was also the right thing to do. These are the companies that are most likely to champion their own programs and challenge the status quo. These are the pioneers who will show the way for others. As my friend Phil Kosak from Carolina Fine Snacks taught me, there will always be plenty of people who want to do "God's work." It is just a question of finding them.

Sometimes we are Peter; more often we are Andrew. We don't need to convince everyone; our story will convince the right ones.

CHAPTER 41

A PLACE TO SUCCEED

THE ANDERSON DISTRIBUTION CENTER achieved all our initial goals. It became our most efficient center in terms of operating costs, quality, and safety. We exceeded our disability hiring goal. We held to our performance standards. But that wasn't all.

Over time, the "No *them*" sign on the wall became a reality. As we began to see people with disabilities as equals, it changed the way we worked. It changed our culture. It changed our work environment. It changed the way we looked at the world.

The main difference between Anderson and other places is that we do more to help people succeed. There is a saying in the autism community: once you've seen one person with autism, you've seen one person with autism. And we've found that to be true about anybody—with or without a disability. We have to treat each person as a unique individual—something we might have given lip service to in a typical work environment but never really would have felt compelled to do. At Anderson, such a focus is a daily necessity.

For one thing, we needed to tailor our approach to motivation.

When we set up monitors with real-time performance information so that team members could tell if they were achieving expectations throughout the day, we thought that would provide enough motivation. This worked for some people, but the monitors weren't enough for others. Some employees, for instance, are motivated by getting a star for each day they perform above standard. One man pastes each star he receives in the spiral notepad he carries in his shirt pocket. He likes getting the stars because they're something tangible—success that he can touch and see.

Managers have learned to listen better because many team members have communication challenges, and words don't always reveal the whole situation. One manager told me, "Not only do I have to listen better to my employees, but I also have to ask myself why they are telling me this and what's going on with them. It has made me a better manager."

We've come to understand that all disabilities are contextual. That is, in certain situations a disability is not a disability. For instance, having only one leg is hardly a disability in playing the violin, but it might be for playing soccer. Even so, we've learned not to make assumptions about what people can or cannot do. It wouldn't surprise me to learn that some one-legged players could make it on a World Cup team. Instead of assuming people can't perform a certain function, we ask them how they would do it. We have been surprised by the effectiveness and simplicity of this approach, and we now include it as a standard methodology that we call ATP (ask the person).

Another key we've discovered in promoting a healthy work environment is to review performance for each employee every week. Not just for the people with disabilities—for everybody. When there's a blip, supervisors look to uncover the cause and work to solve the problem rather than just telling team members to improve or else.

Helping each employee succeed also means acknowledging that not everyone can do the job in the same way. Accommodations mostly consist of simple job aids or tweaks to the equipment. The average cost of each modification is less than twenty-five dollars, and most of them are created using a paper and pencil.

For instance, when an employee with obsessive-compulsive disorder focused so intently on the precise way he opened each case that he started falling behind in productivity, job coach Ben Kelly drew an array of squares on a card to represent the number of cases that needed to be completed in an hour. The team member's focus shifted to checking off boxes on the card, which meant he had to open and process cases faster.

For a custodian who had difficulty remembering each day's assignments, the supervisor prepared a card for each daily task with lists of the steps to be completed. Each day the cards were put in the proper sequence and hooked to the custodian's belt so he would always know what to do and what came next.

Then there was a woman with cerebral palsy whose fingers couldn't reach a recessed button she needed to press to operate a machine. Supervisors placed a socket from a ratchet set around the button and then used a piece cut from a broom handle to raise the button. It worked like a charm.

When manager Rico Robinson was informed that three of the fifteen people who would be driving his forklifts were deaf, his first problem was figuring out how to give instructions to people who couldn't hear. That problem was easily solved—he used scratch pads and phone texts for his own communications, and he made sure his training videos had closed captions. His second concern was that they couldn't drive safely if they couldn't hear whether their horns were working. In a classic example of ATP, he discovered that deaf drivers could check their horns by placing their hands on them and feeling the vibrations when the horn sounded. A more entertaining alternative was to drive up to a group of unsuspecting pedestrians and see if people jumped when they honked.

As we've worked to create a successful environment, we've come to realize that some people with disabilities need help that goes beyond the workplace. Our previous policy had been to discuss issues with the employee only, but now we include family members or other members of an employee's support group. We discovered that some employees, finally able to afford toys such as Xboxes, were going through their own version of adolescent independence—staying up too late and then having difficulty getting to work on time. In years past, we would have considered it the employees' responsibility to manage their time, and if they failed, they would be fired. Now we monitor what's happening at home and try to intervene before the problems get to a crisis point.

People often ask if we pay managers more to do all these things that seem to go far beyond what most managers would do. We don't. These are skills and attitudes they've developed out of necessity: we need to get the job done, and the old ways aren't sufficient. We've had to discover and adapt to new ways of doing things. And since we can't turn our new skills on for one group and off for another, they simply became good habits.

But the benefits haven't been one-way. Managers have seen team members respond with a level of commitment and teamwork they'd never witnessed before. When I asked a group of Anderson managers how they would rate the teamwork in the building on a scale of one to ten, their response was resounding: "Ten."

To get perspective compared to their past experiences, I asked, "How did you rate the teamwork in the other distribution centers when you were working there?"

They settled on the number eight. That didn't seem like much of a difference. I probed a little more.

"And how would you rate them now, after having worked here?"

This time, they came up with "two."

They offered this explanation: "We didn't know what teamwork could be until we worked here."

The work environment has had a profound impact on everyone involved. The satisfaction of our own success doesn't compare to the joy of helping another person be successful. My friend Rob Osmond and I were visiting Anderson recently and overheard Rico talk about how the work had changed him. It hadn't just made him a better manager, he said, but also a better parent, spouse, and friend.

When he comes in to work each day, Rico knows there will be people waiting for him—people who would miss him if he weren't there. He said he knows that's the case because they've told him so. When he leaves work each day and sees the sign at the exit that says, "Thank you for making a difference today," it always makes him look in his rearview mirror at the building behind him and wonder if he did enough for the people who count on him. When asked what made Anderson so special, Rico said matter-of-factly, "What we have here is love."

My friend, a successful businessman, leaned over to me and

said, "That's the first time I have heard *love* used to describe a business workplace."

Greatness is often associated with achievement; it requires continuous energy to maintain and stands at a single point in time. Acts of goodness, in contrast, have a life and an energy of their own and touch others in unpredictable ways.

This was precisely what happened to Rob. A week after his visit to Anderson, he told me about a meeting during which he and his managers were discussing one of their salesmen's poor performance. Usually, he said, these assessments were cut and dried: if a salesman wasn't performing, he'd be replaced. "For the first time ever," Rob said, "I looked around the room and asked, 'What have we done on our part to make him successful?'"

The day-to-day focus at Anderson is about getting the work done, just as it is at any business. Team members tell me the only time they think about disabilities is when a visitor comes. They tend to forget how special the place is. I do too. And sometimes I'm caught by surprise.

Greatness requires continuous energy to maintain and stands at a single point in time. Acts of goodness, in contrast, have a life and an energy of their own and touch others in unpredictable ways.

At one manager's meeting, as I heard managers exchange stories about what they'd done in this or that situation to help someone, their creativity and devotion amazed me. I was struck by how far out of their way these people go, unasked, to make other people successful. As they talked, I was transported back to those conference rooms with teachers during Austin's IEP meetings, shaking hands with each of them and thanking them for what they were doing for my son.

In an instant, I was no longer a senior vice president. I was a parent, like so many other parents who hope and pray their child will someday have a job. I told the managers the story of Austin at the pizza parlor. With my voice occasionally breaking, I told them that I was expressing gratitude on behalf of thousands of parents like me. I thanked them for the difference they were making in other people's lives. I ended with a simple "Thank you, thank you, thank you."

And then I did something I had never done in a business meeting—and haven't done since. I stood there with tears of gratitude running down my cheeks.

As exhilarating as your own success is, it doesn't compare to the joy of helping others succeed. Everybody wins.

x

CHAPTER 42

HOW LONG?

TWO YEARS AFTER we completed the Anderson center, we opened the second distribution center—near Hartford, Connecticut—without a hitch. As it turned out, our goal to have 30 percent of the workforce made up of people with disabilities was too low. At last count, 40 percent of the workforce at Anderson has a disclosed disability; in Hartford, we're at 50 percent. Not only that, but Anderson and Hartford became the most efficient distribution centers in the history of our company. The positive impact we've seen on the culture in Anderson has been replicated in Hartford. Both sites conduct tours and workshops for employers and serve as models for companies that wish to launch their own initiatives.

As for the "one thousand by 2010" goal in the distribution centers, the country's economic recession slowed down our hiring a bit. But we achieved our goal in early 2011, bringing the percentage of people with disabilities in our entire workforce to 10 percent. The measure we'd selected and carefully watched—the percent of new hires—worked: over the last several years, one of three new hires in the entire division was a person with a disability.

When the distribution center managers got together to create a new goal, they set 20 percent of the workforce as the next target to shoot for.

The success in distribution centers was a breakthrough. But what about the stores, where most of the company's employees work? After I made my speech about Anderson at the store managers' meeting in Las Vegas, managers would stop me in the hallways and tell their stories of team members they'd hired in their stores even though we had no specific initiatives in place. I was struck by their passion.

The memory stayed with me. After it was clear that our distribution center initiative would be successful, we charged Deb Russell, the disability hiring expert, with developing an in-store training program. She teamed up with local agencies to build a pool of qualified candidates to fill entry-level positions. When we asked a group of Texas store managers to volunteer to be a part of the initial pilot, we hoped for ten. Thirty-five volunteered on the spot. The stores embraced the program, and word of our success in the Texas stores spread to other parts of the country. Other pilots sprang up in Wisconsin, New York, and Indiana.

The arc of the universe bends toward justice.

One day when Deb was leading a brainstorming session about expanding the pilots, Mark Wagner, the head of stores, dropped by. After listening for a bit, he said to the group, "Why don't we shoot for a target of 10 percent of new hires in our entry-level positions across the entire chain?"

Then Mark left and went to his next meeting. The group was stunned—but also excited. And so began an effort to roll out the plan nationwide. The details would be different from the way things worked at distribution centers because the management structure is different, the jobs are different, and there are more locations. But the heart is the same; the vision is the same. This journey is only beginning, but we are eager to see where it takes us and what we will learn along the way.

As for Austin, the son we thought we had—the one we'd thought had died on the day of his diagnosis—never existed. The son we have is a complete and whole young man. He loves being with people, even though at times he may not talk to them at all and at other times he may talk too much. He laughs a lot—at both appropriate and inappropriate times. He misses people when they're gone too long. He cries when others suffer. He's incapable of hurting another living being.

As I write, Austin is employed part time in a Walgreens retail store near our home. It wasn't long after he started working that we noticed he got up early and left the house thirty minutes before he needed to. We thought it was because he was so eager to get started—a good sign. We later learned that he used most of that time so he could drive an alternate route to work to avoid those dreaded camera-enforced traffic lights. Regardless, he is often at work early.

Does the job matter to Austin? We gave Austin a calendar so he can learn to keep up with his dentist appointments and doctor visits and such. So far it has only two entries for each month: payday and payday.

We know that Austin's story will continue to unfold. There are still worries and uncertainties ahead. But looking back, it's astounding how far Austin has come. Kay and I talk about those days when our dream was that someday Austin would just be considered "weird." Although he has a long way to go, we've been thinking about upgrading that dream to "quirky." He continues to surprise us, so who knows?

And we have come far too. Because of what Austin has taught me—because of the longing he created within me to do the right thing—I saw an opportunity and seized it. I'm grateful that I've gotten to be part of all this. For me and for the countless others who have worked together to make this a success, it has been the best work of our lives. And there is more to do.

When Martin Luther King Jr. stood on the capitol steps of Alabama after the march from Selma to Montgomery in 1965, he said, "I know you are asking today, 'How long will it take? . . . How long will prejudice blind the visions of men, darken their understanding, and drive bright-eyed wisdom from her sacred throne? . . . How long will justice be crucified, and truth bear it?'"

Although he couldn't predict a specific timetable, he could affirm a certainty first observed by abolitionist preacher Theodore Parker, a hundred years before: "How long? Not long, because the arc of the moral universe is long, but it bends toward justice."

Justice. People with disabilities are asking for opportunity. From their standpoint, this is about justice, not charity. And in the end, this isn't just about them; it's also about us. How long before we welcome these individuals fully and embrace them as our own?

They wait for us to recognize their gifts. They wait for us to harness their abilities. They wait for us to value their contributions. How long? Like Martin Luther King Jr., I, too, believe that the arc of the universe bends toward justice.

But it is our hands that must bend it.

Acknowledgments

THIS BOOK BEGAN with a phone call from book agent Scott Mendel after he saw the Anderson story on the nightly news. I was plenty busy and set the idea aside. A few years later, journalist Christine Wicker did a *Parade* magazine article about Anderson and fell in love with the people and the story. It was there that we met, and I helped fill in the details. Afterward she was determined to write a book about what was happening at Walgreens, and in the coming months we stayed in contact as she researched and fleshed out the proposal. When the reception by her publishing contacts was lukewarm, I suggested she call Scott. Although still enthusiastic about the story, he told her it had to be a story told by me. Disappointed, Christine called me with the news. Like so many things I have stumbled across, this was an opportunity that kept popping up until I took action. I suggested that we write it together. Thus began a year of collaborative writing, exchanging ideas, and weaving the story together. I am indebted to Christine for this book; she was my alter ego, writing coach, foil, confidant, and cheerleader as we wrote, revised, and rewrote.

And many thanks to Tyndale House, especially Lisa Jackson and Jon Farrar, who saw that this was more than just a story about hiring people with disabilities. Working with the editorial and marketing staff, I learned the subtleties of publishing terminology. For instance, after delivering the initial manuscript, I learned that "light editing" was editorial speak for "rewrite." I am thankful for the kind and light touch of our editor, Stephanie Rische.

Thanks also to Andrew Hodder-Williams, Tony Collins, and Alison Hull at Lion Hudson, who decided very early to take a leap of faith and publish the UK and Australian edition of this book.

This is the work of many hands. My neighbor Mary and my niece Shelley were excellent in pointing out the rough spots. None worked harder than my older brother, Mickey, a writer who breezed through the final draft and assuaged my concerns by telling me, "You may not write as well as I do, but you tell a good story, and that's enough." He shimmed up several sections, and the Sacagawea chapter is mostly his.

Many thanks to my bosses, who had more faith than fear and never faltered in their support. Thanks to those in the book, named and unnamed, whose stories brought the book to life. Thanks to those on the front lines: Terry Watkins, Dan Coughlin, Sue Thoss, Todd Steffen, and Vinayak Pandit, who led the operations, engineering, and technical teams and never lost sight of the fact that we were putting lightning in a bottle. For everyone named here, there are dozens more who can sleep the sleep of the righteous at night, knowing their work will benefit thousands of others.

Most of all, I thank my wife, Kay. Her simple "Hello, honey!" when she answers my call can turn my whole day around. Her love is lived out in all she does. Thank you, Doris and Bill—you raised a fine daughter. And I agree: I "married up." Thanks to my children, whose lives remind me every day why we want to leave the world a better place. And thanks especially to Austin, with whom I look forward to playing that game of catch on the other side of this life.

I am thankful to all those who fight the good fight in their daily lives and whose deeds go largely unnoticed. Greatness is not measured by the result but in the attempt. As writer Beryl Markham observed seventy years ago in her masterpiece *West with the Night*, "If a man has any greatness in him, it comes to light, not in one flamboyant hour, but in the ledger of his daily work."

PRINCIPLES FOR HIRING PEOPLE WITH DISABILITIES

From 0 to 10 Percent of the Workforce in Four Years

1. Have a champion.

No champion, no success. A champion is the leader of the business unit and has the authority and the drive to make the initiative successful. Champions cannot be conscripted; they must believe in the initiative. A champion covers the backs of the team across the organization and acts and speaks in such a way that subordinates know that employing people with disabilities is a priority, not just a "nice" thing to do. Accountability and authority should flow from the champion down to the rest of the organization where the results are expected. There may be allies from other areas of the business as well, but in times of uncertainty, people look directly above them in the organization.

2. Set a goal and monitor progress relentlessly and conspicuously.

One of the most common sayings in business is "What gets measured gets done." A goal lets people know what success looks like, and monitoring progress in a timely fashion ensures that bumps don't become roadblocks. Develop a key performance indicator (e.g., hire a certain percent of new employees with disabilities by a target date) that is easy to understand and communicates overall progress. Change doesn't come about with a "fire and forget" mentality. Conspicuously refer to progress so others know it's still important to you.

3. Go big.

Create a clear and elevating goal (e.g., 10 percent of new hires, or one thousand people with disabilities in five years). If you can't implement your goal company-wide, apply it to a division or a department or a specific location. Unless you go big, you won't identify the invisible barriers you have in hiring and employing people with disabilities. A large-scale vision, however, will signal that you're serious and will help align the organization. Don't get too hung up on how you're going to measure success, or you'll get distracted. Even getting close to a big goal means you've come a long way from the starting point. By going big, you'll positively impact the culture for both those with disabilities and the typically abled. From there, the movement will grow virally within the company.

4. Have a bias for action, not planning.

Don't spend much time with what-ifs before you get started. If you do, you'll never get started. Plus, you'll never come up with all the potential situations, and many of the problems you anticipate won't happen. You have the skills to fix things as they happen.

5. Don't underestimate the abilities of employees with special needs.

Talent and *disabilities* go in the same sentence. Don't assume that all your requirements are essential for success in the job. Consider them as preferences rather than as absolutes. Not every individual with a disability will be successful, but it will happen more often than you think. If you go the extra mile to help someone be successful and it doesn't work out, you'll be able to sleep at night knowing you gave it your best effort. If you aren't failing every once in a while, you aren't reaching far enough.

6. Apply the same performance standards for all employees.

You're a business, not a charity. People with disabilities can do more than you think (and sometimes more than their advocates think). People want a chance, not a handout; an opportunity, not pity.

7. Keep your fear in check.

The biggest impediment to hiring people with disabilities is fear. Your fear. Human resources' fear. Legal's fear. Operations' fear. There's the fear that people with disabilities can't really do the job. The fear that other team members won't accept them. The fear that they'll get hurt. The fear that insurance or medical costs will rise. The fear of advocacy groups, health and safety, or equal opportunities. The fear of bad press if something goes wrong. And on and on. But the fear can never come close to the sense of accomplishment on the other side.

8. **Start in parts of the organization where the leaders have caught the vision.**

If you begin with leaders who are on board, they will pick up the initiative faster, overcome their fears faster, and be more committed to success. If you begin with leaders who have closed minds, their fears will become self-fulfilling prophecies, and there won't be enough data in the world to change their minds. Goals are achieved most effectively when they're movements of attraction, not coercion. The skeptics will eventually be overcome.

9. **Make sure operations is driving the initiative.**

If your organization were a football team, the CEO would be the coach, operations would be the ball carrier, and human resources/legal would be the front line that removes barriers along the way. Without the commitment of operations, there's no success. Period. If people are spending more effort identifying risk than mitigating it, you'll never make progress.

10. **Adapt a "consistent in objective, flexible in means" attitude toward policies.**

If current policies and procedures were adequate, more people with disabilities would already be in the workforce. Policies that we accept as typical practice can create barriers to employing talented and productive individuals with disabilities (e.g., excluding applicants with gaps on their résumés, requiring job applicants to answer prescreening questions online). Be open to change when a policy or process gets in the way of your objective.

RANDY LEWIS

11. **Manage in the gray.**

Most people like black-and-white policies because they are consistent and easy to administer. However, such policies may get in the way of a work environment where each person is treated as an individual and where that person's circumstances are considered in each decision. Adapt a "consistent in objective, flexible in means" attitude. Think principles, not rules. Be willing to overturn or modify rules as particular situations arise. It's scary but invigorating when leaders learn to manage in the gray.

12. **Provide visible support from the top.**

Offer cover for those who are responsible for the success of the program. Let them know that if they make mistakes trying to do the right thing, you have their backs. We all make mistakes. Then we correct those mistakes. Your people need to know that you expect them to give their best thinking and efforts.

13. **Use community partners.**

Get help to find, screen, and train people with disabilities. Community partners often have funding for these activities. If you wait for people with disabilities to find you on their own, you'll be disappointed. The status quo is a heavy impediment to overcome for both employers who believe people with disabilities are unemployable and potential employees who fear discrimination.

14. **Develop a transitional work program.**

People with disabilities may learn differently or take longer to develop the necessary skills, so your normal

221

procedures for training new employees may have hidden barriers. Consider creating a transitional work program as an additional pipeline into the company. The transitional work program may include supports such as community partners that will find, screen, and train employees and job coaches and offer them support as they progress on the job. Flexible timelines will also help people continue to progress in reaching job standards and gaining the necessary skills. Outside financial assistance and alternative pay structures for those in the program can be used to offset any incremental costs of the transitional work group, if necessary.

15. **Unleash people's longing to make a difference.**

Deep down everyone wants to do something important and leave the world a better place. Let team members know their part is critical. Remind them that this is good for the business, but it's also a game changer for how business is done. And they are paving the way.

16. **When you are successful, give it away.**

Hiring people with disabilities is the smart thing to do from a business perspective. It results in effective employees and a better work culture. Once you have reached a level of success, share your story and what you've learned with other departments and other businesses—even your competitors. This work isn't only important for the business; it's important for all of us. This may be the most satisfying work of your life. Pass it on.

MOVING FROM GRIEF TO ACCEPTANCE

Perspectives from the Parent of a Child with a Disability

1. The grieving may take longer than you expect.

There will be good days and bad days, and the bad days will sneak up on you. You'll find yourself breaking down or fighting to hold it together at the most unexpected times—perhaps when some small thing happens or when someone says something ill considered. Some days will just be dreary. Be patient with yourself—the pain will ease. It may seem unendurable and endless, but it will ease.

2. Don't be too hard on yourself.

Guilt is grieving's ugly stepchild. Again and again, you'll wonder, *What did I do to cause this?* You did nothing wrong. Again and again, you'll ask, *Why can't I be stronger?* You're strong enough.

3. Lean on others.

Accept the help and encouragement of friends, support groups, and other parents in similar circumstances. If you are a person of faith, draw strength from that. You may even discover that your faith is strengthened in the process.

4. It won't be overwhelming forever.

The first years after Austin's diagnosis, I worried about him about every ten seconds. *Has he gotten out of the house? What are we going to do?* Those or similar thoughts still cycle with regularity, but over time the intervals have become longer.

5. Most dreaded scenarios won't happen.

I saw a story on TV about a boy with autism who had been found after wandering off from camp and spending the night alone in the woods during a thunderstorm. The reporter asked the mom if she had been worried about him being struck by lightning. She replied, "No, because that would be like lightning striking twice."

6. People will be awkward around your child.

Some people ignore Austin; others treat him as if he understands everything. People's discomfort usually stems from the fear of doing something wrong. Help them navigate the unknown terrain by modeling appropriate behavior through your words and actions.

7. Work for affordable treatment and therapies.

Companies and governments try hard to reduce medical costs. One way insurance companies keep benefits low is by making you jump through hoops with paperwork and by denying claims. Join with other employees to bring such issues to light. Then keep at it.

8. Work with your child on the little things.

Putting effort into daily activities like healthy eating and hygiene will pay large rewards later. The effort you spend now is ten times less than it will be if you have to start from scratch later.

9. Teach your child how to do jobs around the house.

Find responsibilities that are appropriate for your child, such as making the bed, washing the dishes, or taking out the trash. It takes lots of patience and effort, and in the short run it's easier and faster to do it yourself. But success is a delight worth waiting for—plus, you'll learn a lot about your child in the process.

10. Don't forget the rest of the family.

The needs of a child with a disability are obvious and can become the focus of all your energy. But other family members have needs too. Don't overlook them.

11. Raise your expectations.

If you don't have high expectations, why should anyone else? Everyone who works with your child wants him or her to be successful. Help them see the possibilities.

12. Expect the system to provide integration, employment, and independence, not lifelong welfare and poverty.

Secondary schools have resources for helping students get into their choice of colleges; schools should also help place students who don't go to college into decent jobs.

13. Don't focus on your child's specific disability when advocating for change.

The barriers to employment and services usually apply

to all disabilities. Join with others for institutional change. Getting the door to open is more important than who gets in first.

14. At times you will get frustrated when helping your child fit into this world.

The enemy is ignorance and fear, not malicious intent. Resistance will be overcome by love and knowledge. Channel your pain and anger into resolve and resilience.

15. As a parent of a child with a disability, you have been conscripted into a role that few would ever volunteer for.

You will be a teacher, comforter, protector, and advocate. You are not alone. According to the Centers for Disease Control and Prevention, every year in the United States another six hundred thousand families will have a child born with a developmental disability. Feel their pain—and feel their power. What you do with them is up to you.

And finally, here is the best advice we ever got. When Austin entered the school system at age three, Kay was overwhelmed thinking about what she should be doing to ensure the best outcome for Austin. She met with the school psychologist and shared her concerns. The psychologist put her hand on Kay's arm and said, "The data shows that the kids that do the best are those with strong relationships. Go home and love your son."

Notes

CHAPTER 14: PICK YOUR MOMENT

1. Seamus Heaney, *The Cure at Troy: A Version of Sophocles' Philoctetes* (New York: Farrar, Straus and Giroux, 1961), 77.

CHAPTER 18: MANAGE YOUR FEAR

1. Centers for Disease Control and Prevention, "National Center on Birth Defects and Developmental Disabilities," August 14, 2012, http://www.cdc.gov/ncbddd /features/counting-autism.html.

CHAPTER 27: DON'T LET THE BIG ONE GET AWAY

1. US Census Bureau, www.census.gov/prod/2011pubs/p60-239.pdf.

CHAPTER 40: BEING ANDREW

1. James P. Kaletta, Douglas J. Binks, and Richard Robinson, "Creating an Inclusive Workplace: Integrating Employees with Disabilities into a Distribution Center Environment," American Society of Safety Engineers, *Professional Safety*, June 2012, www.asse.org/professionalsafety/pastiss ues/057/06/062_071_F1Ka_0612.pdf.

About the Author

As senior vice president, RANDY LEWIS oversaw Walgreens' supply chain for sixteen years as the company grew from 1,500 stores to 8,000—with the most advanced logistics network in the industry. Lewis pioneered a disability employment model in the distribution centers that is changing the lives of thousands and serves as a model for other companies around the world.

Throughout his career, Lewis has striven to live out his belief that excellence, people, and community are the cornerstones of business leadership. Both in the United States and internationally, he has shared the story of how applying these principles can both improve performance and benefit the community.

In addition to having been recognized for his contributions to the field of logistics, he was recognized as Leader of the Year for outstanding service to the field of human resources and business by the Human Resources Management Association of Chicago. He received South Carolina's highest award to non-citizens, the Order of the Silver Crescent, for his leadership and his contributions to the well-being of its citizenry.

He and his wife, Kay, have three children and live in the Chicago area with their son, Austin.

Learn more at NoGreatnessWithoutGoodness.com.

READ THIS AND DO GOOD

The author will donate all his proceeds from this book according to readers' preference of charity.

Go to www.nogreatnesswithoutgoodness.com to learn more.